EXPLORING
ENGLISH

3

EXPLORING ENGLISH

3

Tim Harris • Allan Rowe

Longman

Exploring English 3

Copyright © 1995 by Addison-Wesley Publishing Company, Inc.

Longman, 10 Bank Street, White Plains, NY 10606

Editorial director: Joanne Dresner
Acquisitions editor: Anne Boynton-Trigg
Production editor: Nik Winter
Text design: Curt Belshe
Cover design: Curt Belshe
Cover illustration: Allan Rowe

ISBN 0-201-82577-5

Library of Congress Cataloging-in-Publication Data

Harris, Tim.
    Exploring English / Tim Harris; illustrated by Allan Rowe.
        p.   cm.
    1. English language—Textbooks for foreign speakers.   I. Rowe,
Allan.   II. Title.
PE1128.H347   1995
428.2'4—dc20   94-47408
                                                               CIP

1 2 3 4 5 6 7 8 9 10-BAM-99 98 97 96 95

To our families

Contents

Preface

Exploring English is a comprehensive, six-level course for adult and young adult students of English. It teaches all four language skills—listening, speaking, reading, and writing—with an emphasis on oral communication. The course combines a strong grammar base with in-depth coverage of language functions and life skills.

Exploring English:

Teaches grammar inductively. The basic structures are introduced in context through illustrated situations and dialogues. Students use the structures in talking about the situations and re-enacting the dialogues. They encounter each structure in a variety of contexts, including practice exercises, pair work activities, and readings. This repeated exposure enables students to make reliable and useful generalizations about the language. They develop a "language sense"—a feeling for words—that carries over into their daily use of English.

Includes language functions in every chapter from beginning through advanced levels. Guided conversations, discussions, and role plays provide varied opportunities to practice asking for and giving information, expressing likes and dislikes, agreeing and disagreeing, and so on.

Develops life skills in the areas most important to students: food, clothing, transportation, work, housing, and health care. Everyday life situations provide contexts for learning basic competencies: asking directions, taking a bus, buying food, shopping for clothes, and so on. Students progress from simpler tasks, such as describing occupations at the beginning level, to interviewing for jobs and discussing problems at work at more advanced levels.

Incorporates problem solving and critical thinking in many of the lessons, especially at the intermediate and advanced levels. The stories in *Exploring English* present a cast of colorful characters who get involved in all kinds of life problems, ranging from personal relationships to work-related issues to politics. Students develop critical-thinking skills as they discuss these problems, give their opinions, and try to find solutions. These discussions also provide many opportunities for students to talk about their own lives.

Provides extensive practice in listening comprehension through illustrated situations. Students are asked to describe each illustration in their own words before listening to the accompanying story (which appears on the reverse side of the page). Then they answer questions based on the story, while looking at the illustration. The students respond to what they see and hear without referring to a text, just as they would in actual conversation.

Offers students frequent opportunities for personal expression. The emphasis throughout *Exploring English* is on communication—encouraging students to use the language to express their own ideas and feelings. Free response questions in Books 1 and 2 give students the opportunity to talk about themselves using simple, straightforward English. Every chapter in Books 3–6 has a special section, called "One Step Further," that includes discussion topics such as work, leisure activities, cinema, travel, dating, and marriage. Ideas for role plays are also provided to give additional opportunities for free expression. The general themes are familiar to students because they draw on material already covered in the same chapter. Role plays give students a chance to interact spontaneously— perhaps the most important level of practice in developing communication skills.

Provides continuous review and reinforcement. Each chapter concludes with a review section and every fourth chapter is devoted entirely to review, allowing students to practice newly acquired language in different combinations.

Provides exposure to key structures that students will be learning at the next level. This material, included in a special unit called "Preview," can be introduced at any time during the course at the discretion of the teacher.

Presents attractive art that visually supports and is integral with the language being taught. Humorous and imaginative illustrations, in full color, make *Exploring English* fun for students. In addition, the richness of the art allows teachers to devise their own spin-off activities, increasing the teachability of each page.

Each volume of *Exploring English* is accompanied by a Workbook. The Workbook lessons are closely coordinated with the lessons in the Student Book. They provide additional writing practice using the same grammatical structures and vocabulary while expanding on basic functions and life skills. The activities range from sentence completion exercises to guided paragraph and composition writing.

Student Books and Workbooks include clear labels and directions for each activity. In addition, Teacher's Resource Manuals are available for each level. These Manuals provide step-by-step guidance for teaching each page, expansion activities, and answers to the exercises. Each student page is reproduced for easy reference.

Audiocassettes for each level featuring an entertaining variety of native voices round out the series. All of the dialogues, readings, and pronunciation exercises are included on the tapes.

Chapter 1

TOPICS
Food
Music
At the park

GRAMMAR
A lot/much/many
A little/a few

FUNCTIONS
Talking about quantity
Telling a story
Giving opinions

1

2

1. *Talk about the pictures.*
2. *Listen to the stories.*
3. *Answer the story questions.*

READING

1 Sam Brown is a shoe repairman. He has a lot of customers and a lot of work, so he never has much free time. Sam works hard and repairs a lot of shoes, but he doesn't make much money. That's because his prices are very low. Sam doesn't think money is very important.

1. What is Sam's job?
2. Does he have much work?
3. What about free time?
4. Does Sam make much money?
5. Are his prices high or low?
6. Does Sam think money is important?

2 Johnnie Wilson is the owner of a bookshop. He has a lot of books on history and philosophy, but not many books on science or medicine. Normally, Johnnie doesn't have many customers because his books are very expensive. But today he's having a sale and there are a lot of people in his shop.

1. What kind of shop does Johnnie have?
2. Does he have many books on history and philosophy?
3. What about science and medicine?
4. Does Johnnie normally have many customers?
5. What about today?

QUANTIFIERS: Affirmative
Johnnie has a lot of books.
_____ magazines.
_____ postcards.
_____ paper.

PRACTICE • *Make sentences with **a lot of**.*

Dr. Pasto is very popular.
He has a lot of friends.

He speaks nine languages.
He speaks a lot of languages.

1. He has a dozen dictionaries.
2. He collects hundreds of butterflies.
3. He often drinks tea.
4. Mr. Bascomb has fourteen employees.
5. He's a rich man.
6. He knows everyone in town.
7. He has a large library.
8. Jimmy and Linda are very popular.
9. They often buy magazines.

Listen and practice.

MR. BASCOMB: My shoes look good, Sam.

SAM BROWN: Thank you, Mr. Bascomb.

MR. BASCOMB: How much money do I owe you?

SAM BROWN: Four dollars and fifty cents.

MR. BASCOMB: That isn't much.

SAM BROWN: It's a lot of money for some people.

JIMMY: I saw Bonnie yesterday. She didn't look very well.

LINDA: She has a lot of problems, Jimmy.

JIMMY: Does Bonnie have many friends?

LINDA: No, she doesn't have very many.

JIMMY: Does she ever go out and have fun?

LINDA: No, not very often. It's a shame.

PAIR WORK • *Ask and answer questions about the pictures.*

1. friends
A: **Does Linda have many friends?**
B: **Yes, she does. (She has a lot of friends.)**
A: **Does Bonnie have many friends?**
B: **No, she doesn't.**

2. free time
A: **Does Sam have much free time?**
B: **No, he doesn't.**
A: **Does Jack have much free time?**
B: **Yes, he does. (He has a lot of free time.)**

3. customers

4. money

5. food

6. apples

7. chickens

8. water

1. *Talk about the pictures.*
2. *Listen to the stories.*
3. *Answer the story questions.*

READING

1 Jack Grubb is the owner of a popular snack bar. He's a good guy, but he's lazy. He works only a few hours a day. Jack usually has a lot of customers, but tonight there's a football game and a lot of his regular customers went to see it. There are only a few people in Jack's snack bar at the moment.

1. Who's the man behind the counter?
2. Is he the owner of a restaurant or a snack bar?
3. Does he work hard?
4. Does he usually have many customers?
5. What about tonight?
6. Where did Jack's regular customers go?

2 Barbara and Tino are having breakfast at Joe's Coffee Shop. Tino has a big appetite, and he's eating a lot this morning. He's having bacon and eggs, three slices of bread, a cup of coffee, and an apple. Barbara isn't very hungry. She's only having some coffee for breakfast. She likes her coffee with a little sugar.

1. Where are Barbara and Tino having breakfast?
2. How much is Tino eating?
3. What's he having this morning?
4. Is Barbara hungry?
5. What's she having for breakfast?
6. How does she like her coffee?

COUNTABLES
Jack is talking to a few customers.
_____ friends.
_____ people.
_____ men.

UNCOUNTABLES
She likes her coffee with a little sugar.
_____ cream.
_____ milk.

PRACTICE • *Make sentences using **a little** and **a few**.*

knives
There are a few knives on the shelf.

flour
There's a little flour on the shelf.

1. sugar
2. glasses
3. dishes
4. coffee
5. tea
6. bottles
7. jam
8. forks
9. spoons

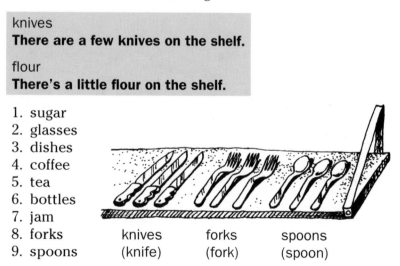

knives   forks   spoons
(knife)   (fork)   (spoon)

Listen and practice.

JENNY: You're doing a good job, Marty.

MARTY: Thanks, Jenny. Can you give me a little help?

JENNY: Sure. Do you have another brush?

MARTY: Yes. Here's a brush and a bucket of paint.

JENNY: Marty, there's only a little paint left in the bucket.

MARTY: Don't worry. There's more paint in the wagon.

JENNY: What else do you have in the wagon?

MARTY: Just some old comic books.

JENNY: Can I borrow a few of your comic books?

MARTY: OK, but take only a few. I don't have very many.

JENNY: Gee, these are really good! I like this story about Superman.

MARTY: Jenny, are you going to help me or not?

JENNY: Sure, but I can stay only a few more minutes. My mother is waiting for me.

PRACTICE • *Describe these pictures using **a lot of, only a little,** and **only a few.***

1. letters/mail box
There are a lot of letters in the mail box.

2. gas/tank
There's only a little gas in the tank.

3. cars/parking lot
There are only a few cars in the parking lot.

4. books/bookcase

5. coffee/pot

6. salad/bowl

7. apples/box

8. orange juice/bottle

9. cherries/dish

10. lemonade/pitcher

11. ice cream/carton

12. people/restaurant

PAIR WORK • *Ask and answer questions about the pictures.*

1. letters/mail box
A: **How many letters are in the mail box?**
B: **A lot.**

2. gas/tank
A: **How much gas is in the tank?**
B: **Just a little.**

3. cars/parking lot
A: **How many cars are in the parking lot?**
B: **Just a few.**

Mr. Bascomb is a good musician. He can play the piano and the violin. He loves classical music and plays a lot of compositions by Mozart. On Saturday afternoons, he practices with his friends. They play well together, but they don't have much time for their music. They're all busy people. At the moment, Mrs. Bascomb is serving them tea and cookies.

"Do you want a little milk with your tea, Dr. Pasto?"

"Yes, please, Mrs. Bascomb."

"How many times are you going to play the same music?"

"We're going to play it a lot," says Mr. Bascomb. "Practice makes perfect."

Mrs. Bascomb has an unhappy look on her face. "Why don't you play something different?"

"Good idea," says Dr. Pasto. "How about a little jazz?"

"I don't care much for jazz," says Mr. Bascomb. "But it's better than rock. Anything's better than rock."

"Don't be a snob, dear," says Mrs. Bascomb.

Dr. Pasto smiles. "In my opinion, there are only two kinds of music — good music and bad music."

"I agree," says Mr. Bascomb. "Classical music is good — and everything else is bad."

STORY QUESTIONS

1. Is Mr. Bascomb a good musician?
2. What instruments can he play?
3. What kind of music does he like?
4. What does Mr. Bascomb do on Saturday afternoons?
5. Do Mr. Bascomb and his friends have much time for their music? Why not?
6. What is Mrs. Bascomb serving them?
7. Why is she unhappy?
8. Do you think Mr. Bascomb is a snob? Why?
9. What is Dr. Pasto's opinion about music?
10. What does Mr. Bascomb say?
11. What do you think?

PRACTICE • *Describe what's in the refrigerator using **a lot of, only a little,** and **only a few.***

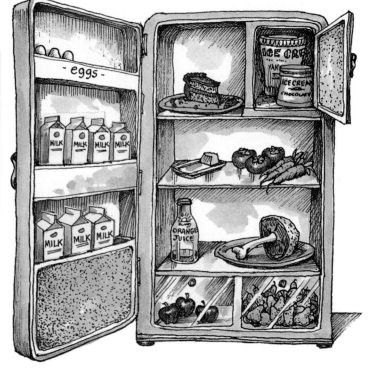

milk
There's a lot of milk in the refrigerator.

orange juice
There's only a little orange juice in the refrigerator.

carrots
There are only a few carrots in the refrigerator.

1. ham
2. tomatoes
3. cake
4. ice cream
5. apples
6. pears
7. eggs
8. butter

FREE RESPONSE

1. What do you have in your refrigerator?
2. How often do you go to the market?
3. Do you always make a shopping list?
4. What kind of food do you like?
5. Do you eat much fruit? vegetables?
6. What do you usually have for breakfast?
7. What kind of desserts do you like?
8. How often do you eat out?
9. What's your favorite restaurant?

GROUP WORK • *You and your friends have thirty dollars to buy some food for dinner. What kind of food are you going to buy? Talk about it and make a shopping list.*

PRACTICE • *Make a sentence for each picture using **a lot of, much,** and **many.***

1. people/bus stop
There are a lot of people at the bus stop.

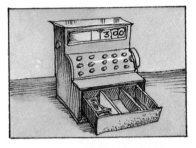

2. money/cash register
There isn't much money in the cash register.

3. cookies/plate
There aren't many cookies on the plate.

4. mustard/jar

5. food/table

6. people/party

7. stamps/envelope

8. eggs/basket

9. soup/pot

10. people/meeting

11. magazines/desk

12. perfume/bottle

PAIR WORK • *Ask and answer questions about the pictures.*

1. people/bus stop
A: **How many people are at the bus stop?**
B: **A lot.**

2. money/cash register
A: **How much money is in the cash register?**
B: **Just a little.**

3. cookies/plate
A: **How many cookies are on the plate?**
B: **Just a few.**

PAIR WORK 1 • *Ask and answer questions.*

> write/letters
> A: **Do you write many letters?**
> B: **Yes, I write a lot of letters.**
> OR **No, I don't write many letters. (I write very few letters.)**
>
> have/free time
> A: **Do you have much free time?**
> B: **Yes, I have a lot of free time.**
> OR **No, I don't have much free time. (I have very little free time.)**

1. have/work
2. have/fun
3. see/movies
4. read/books
5. do/homework
6. get/letters
7. buy/food
8. eat/fruit
9. drink/milk
10. play/sports
11. meet/interesting people
12. know/artists

PAIR WORK 2 • *Ask and answer questions.*

> 1. a pencil
> A: **How much is a pencil?**
> B: **About fifty cents.**

1. a pencil   2. a light bulb   3. a cup of coffee   4. a loaf of bread

5. a comb   6. a toothbrush   7. an apple   8. an ice cream cone

9. a newspaper   10. an umbrella   11. a bag of peanuts   12. a bag of popcorn

FREE RESPONSE

1. Are you enjoying your English class?
2. How do you come to class?
3. Are you living with your family?
4. How many brothers and sisters do you have? What do they do?
5. What do you and your friends like to do when you're together?
6. What did you do yesterday? Did you have a good time?
7. What time did you go to bed last night? Did you sleep well?
8. When did you leave your home this morning? Did you take the bus?
9. What are you going to do tonight? this weekend?

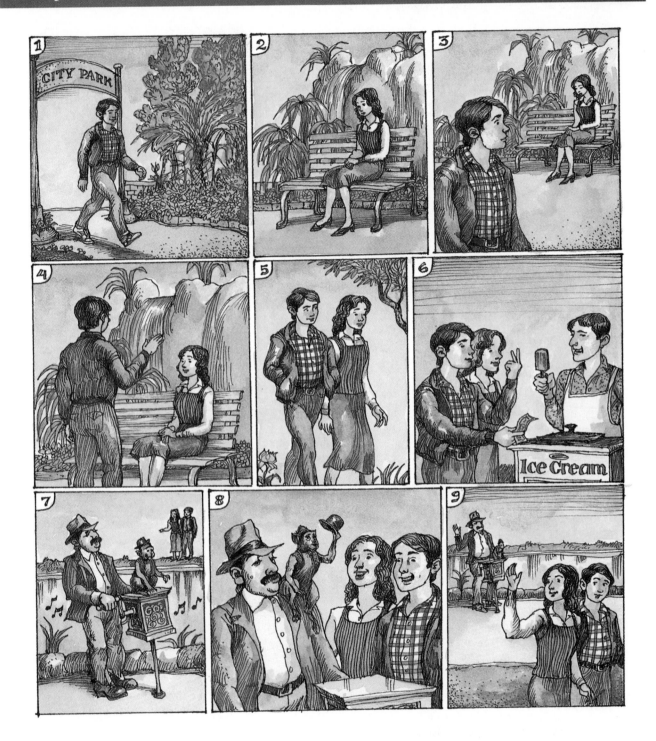

GROUP WORK • *Tell the story of Jimmy and Bonnie and the organ grinder. One student describes the first picture, another student describes the second picture, and so on. For example:*

Student A: **Jimmy is walking in the park. He looks happy. It's a beautiful day.**

COMPOSITION • *Write a short composition about Jimmy and Bonnie. Give some details. What kind of day is it? Is Jimmy in a good mood? What about Bonnie?*

1. Bonnie (make–made)

A: **Why is Bonnie happy?**
B: **She's happy because she made a new friend.**

2. Fred (find–found)

3. Marty (catch–caught)

4. Stanley (sell–sold)

Thank you, Tino.

5. Barbara (bring–brought)

Linda, this is Bob.

BOB!

6. Linda (call–called)

I got an A on my test!

7. Jenny (get–got)

SCORE
B N
98 46

8. Jimmy (win–won)

Classical

Jazz

Rock   Country

TALKING ABOUT MUSIC

1. What kind of music do you like?
2. Do you play a musical instrument?
3. Who's your favorite singer?
4. What's your favorite group?
5. What kind of music is popular in your country?
6. What kind of music is good for dancing?
7. Where is a good place to hear music in your city?

GROUP WORK • *Talk about music with other students in your class.*

COMPOSITION • *Write about a famous singer, musician, or musical group. Why are they popular? Describe their music.*

GRAMMAR SUMMARY

QUANTIFIERS: Affirmative

He has	a lot of	money.
		friends.

Negative

He doesn't have	much money.
	many friends.

Interrogative

Does he have	much money?
	many friends?

COUNTABLES AND UNCOUNTABLES

They have	a lot of	sugar.	They have	a little sugar.
		oranges.		a few oranges.

HOW MUCH/HOW MANY

How much sugar	do they have?
How many oranges	

Chapter

TOPICS
Seasons
Weather
Birthdays
Leisure activities
At the bank
Movies

GRAMMAR
Ordinal numbers
Present continuous for future
Some/any compounds
Must (logical conclusion)

FUNCTIONS
Inquiring about intention
Making suggestions
Making logical conclusions
Giving opinions

Summer   June 21–September 20

Fall   September 21–December 20

Winter   December 21–March 20

Spring   March 21–June 20

In the northern part of the United States, the weather changes dramatically from one season to the next. In the summer it's usually hot and sunny. In the fall the weather gets cooler, and the leaves change colors. In the winter it gets cold, and there's often a lot of snow. In the spring the weather gets warmer, and the flowers begin to bloom. Many people think that spring is the most beautiful time of the year.

TALKING ABOUT THE WEATHER

1. When is the weather hot and sunny in the northern part of the United States?
2. Does the weather get warmer or cooler in the fall?
3. When does the weather get cold?
4. What happens in the spring?
5. Does the weather in your country change dramatically from season to season?
6. Is there a big difference between the weather in your country and the weather in the United States?
7. What kind of weather do you like?
8. What is your favorite season? Why?
9. What do you like to do in the summer? in the winter?

NEW VOCABULARY

Listen and repeat.

MONTHS OF THE YEAR

January	April	July	October
February	May	August	November
March	June	September	December

ORDINAL NUMBERS

1st	first	11th	eleventh	21st	twenty-first
2nd	second	12th	twelfth	22nd	twenty-second
3rd	third	13th	thirteenth	23rd	twenty-third
4th	fourth	14th	fourteenth	24th	twenty-fourth
5th	fifth	15th	fifteenth	25th	twenty-fifth
6th	sixth	16th	sixteenth	26th	twenty-sixth
7th	seventh	17th	seventeenth	27th	twenty-seventh
8th	eighth	18th	eighteenth	28th	twenty-eighth
9th	ninth	19th	nineteenth	29th	twenty-ninth
10th	tenth	20th	twentieth	30th	thirtieth

TALKING ABOUT DATES

1. What is the date today?
2. When is the first day of summer? winter?
3. When is New Year's Day?
4. What is your favorite holiday? When is it?

TALKING ABOUT BIRTHDAYS

1. When is your birthday?
2. When is your mother's birthday? your father's birthday?
3. How do people celebrate birthdays in your country?
4. What kind of presents do you like to give to your friends on their birthdays?
5. How do you like to celebrate your birthday?

Rio de Janeiro

Dr. Pasto was in South America last March. Here is his travel itinerary.

MARCH						
Sunday	**Monday**	**Tuesday**	**Wednesday**	**Thursday**	**Friday**	**Saturday**
			1 *Bogotá*	2	3	4 *Quito*
5	6	7 *Lima*	8	9 *La Paz*	10	11
12 *Santiago*	13	14	15 *Buenos Aires*	16	17	18 *São Paulo*
19	20 *Rio de Janeiro*	21	22	23 *Brasília*	24	25
26 *Caracas*	27	28 *Panama City*	29	30	31	

PAIR WORK • *Ask and answer questions about Dr. Pasto's trip.*

A: **When was Dr. Pasto in Bogotá?**
B: **He was in Bogotá on March first, second, and third.**

1. When was he in Quito?
2. When was he in Lima?
3. When was he in La Paz?
4. When was he in Santiago?
5. When was he in Buenos Aires?

6. When was he in São Paulo?
7. When was he in Rio de Janeiro?
8. When was he in Brasília?
9. When was he in Caracas?
10. When was he in Panama City?

Listen and practice.

JOHNNIE: Hi, Maria. What are you doing tonight?

MARIA: I'm seeing a movie with Peter.

JOHNNIE: Are you meeting him at the theater?

MARIA: No, we're going in his car.

JOHNNIE: What are you doing after the movie?

MARIA: We're having dinner at a Mexican restaurant.

JOHNNIE: Well, have a good time.

MARIA: Thanks, Johnnie. See you later.

PRESENT CONTINUOUS for the FUTURE

They're meeting their friends tonight.

_____ attending a lecture _____.

_____ going to the movies _____.

_____ eating out _____.

PAIR WORK • *Look at Peter's schedule for Friday. Ask and answer questions about what he's doing at different hours of the day.*

7:30—Take car to garage

A: **What's he doing at seven-thirty?**

B: **He's taking his car to the garage.**

FREE RESPONSE

What are you doing after class?

I'm meeting a friend.   (going to the library, etc.)

1. What are you doing tonight?
2. Are you eating out tonight?
3. What are you doing tomorrow morning?
4. Are you getting up early tomorrow?
5. What are you doing tomorrow afternoon?
6. Are you going out tomorrow night?
7. Are you going out Friday night?
8. What are you doing this Saturday?
9. Are you going to a movie this weekend?

Listen and practice.

PAIR WORK • *Have similar conversations. The sweets can come from a wife, husband, girlfriend, boyfriend, etc.*

1. box of chocolates

2. box of doughnuts

3. bag of cookies

4. bag of cupcakes

5. box of apple tarts

6. box of candies

Listen and practice.

BOB: Hi, Linda. Are you waiting for someone?

LINDA: No, I'm not waiting for anyone.

BOB: Good. Let's go somewhere.

LINDA: Where do you want to go?

BOB: Anywhere. How about the zoo?

LINDA: That sounds like fun. We can look at the wild animals, and feed them too.

BOB: And we can have some popcorn and peanuts.

LINDA: Come on. Let's go.

PAIR WORK • *Have similar conversations about the pictures below. Talk about what you can do at these places.*

1. park

2. beach

3. Disco Club*

4. Main Street*

*You can suggest any popular club or street where you live.

CONVERSATION

Listen and practice.

MABEL: Where's your friend Jack? I hardly ever see him.

SAM: He's always at the library.

MABEL: He must read a lot.

SAM: He does. And he can discuss anything.

MABEL: He must be intelligent.

SAM: He is. But he doesn't like to work.

MABEL: He must be lazy, too.

<table>
<tr><td colspan="2" align="center">Must be + adjective</td></tr>
<tr><td>Jack can discuss anything.
Nancy _____.
They _____.
You _____.</td><td>He must be intelligent.
She _____.
They _____.
You _____.</td></tr>
</table>

PRACTICE • *Make sentences with **must be** + adjective.*

Sam worked very hard today.
He must be tired.

Tino can lift anything.
He must be strong.

1. Jack doesn't like to work.
2. Barney found a ten-dollar bill.
3. Maria lost her handbag.
4. Everyone likes Dr. Pasto.
5. Anne takes three showers a day.
6. Mr. Bascomb didn't go to work today.
7. Albert is having three hamburgers for lunch.
8. He wants five glasses of milk.
9. Ula Hackey has a big house, two cars, and a lot of expensive clothes.

<table>
<tr><td colspan="2" align="center">Must + verb + a lot</td></tr>
<tr><td>They're always at school.
_____ at the office.
_____ in the kitchen.
_____ on the telephone.</td><td>They must study a lot.
_____ work _____.
_____ cook _____.
_____ talk _____.</td></tr>
</table>

PRACTICE • *Make sentences with **must** + verb + **a lot**.*

Fred is always in bed.
He must sleep a lot.

Otis and Gloria often go to the club.
They must dance a lot.

1. Jack is always at the library.
2. Mr. Bascomb is always at the office.
3. Barbara is a good tennis player.
4. Nancy is a good pilot.
5. Peter knows Europe very well.
6. Albert is very fat.
7. Mrs. Brown is always in the kitchen.
8. Linda is always on the telephone.
9. The children are always in the park.

Mr. Bascomb likes to save money, so he usually walks to work. Last Friday, however, he was late, so he called a cab. A few minutes later, a taxi pulled up in front of his house. Mr. Bascomb kissed his wife good-bye and got in the taxi. The driver was Barney Field.

"Hello," he said. "Aren't you Mr. Bascomb, president of City Bank?"

"That's right," said Mr. Bascomb. "How did you know?"

"I saw your picture in the newspaper," said Barney. "You're a very important man."

"Thank you," said Mr. Bascomb, smiling. "What's your name?"

"Barney Field. I'm very glad to meet you, sir. I went to your bank every day last week."

"You did?"

"Yes, sir. I want to borrow some money."

"Oh really," said Mr. Bascomb. "What do you want the money for?"

"I want to fix up my cab," said Barney. "It doesn't run very well. The engine makes a lot of noise. It's bad for business."

"That's true," said Mr. Bascomb. "I can see you have a problem."

On the way to the bank, Mr. Bascomb talked to Barney. He liked Barney's friendly personality and careful driving. When the cab pulled up in front of the bank, Mr. Bascomb got out and talked to the driver.

"Barney, I like you. I'm going to give you the money. How much do you need?"

"About five hundred dollars."

"OK," said Mr. Bascomb, "Come and see me at the bank on Monday."

Barney was very happy. "Thank you very much, Mr. Bascomb," he said. "There's just one thing."

"Yes, Barney, what is it?"

"You owe me $5.25 for taxi fare."

"But Barney," said Mr. Bascomb, "I'm going to loan you $500, and you're worried about $5.25."

Barney smiled. "I know, Mr. Bascomb, but do you want to loan your money to a bad businessman?"

STORY QUESTIONS

1. Why does Mr. Bascomb usually walk to work?
2. Why did he call a cab last Friday?
3. Who was the driver?
4. How did Barney know that Mr. Bascomb was president of City Bank?
5. Why does Barney want to borrow money from the bank?
6. What's wrong with Barney's cab?
7. How much does Barney need for repairs?
8. What does Mr. Bascomb like about Barney?
9. Is he going to give Barney the money?
10. Do you think Barney is a good businessman? Why?

CONVERSATION

Listen and practice.

FREE RESPONSE • *Answer the questions using one of these expressions:* ***I think so, I don't think so, I hope so, I hope not.***

1. Is Barney a good businessman?
2. Is he going to be rich some day?
3. Are you going to be famous?
4. Are you going to travel this year?
5. Are you going to study another language?
6. Is this class going to end soon?
7 Is the weather going to be hot next week?
8. Is it going to rain tomorrow?
9. Are you going to have a good time this weekend?

🎧 *Listen and practice.*

MR. BASCOMB: What can I do for you?

MS. BUTZ: I need to borrow some money. Fast.

MR. BASCOMB: What is it for?

MS. BUTZ: I want to *buy a new car.*

MR. BASCOMB: How much do you need?

MS. BUTZ: *Nine thousand dollars.*

MR. BASCOMB: Are you employed?

MS. BUTZ: Yes. I work *at a beauty salon.*

MR. BASCOMB: Good. Maybe I can help you.

MS. BUTZ: I hope so. I really want to buy a new car.

PAIR WORK • *Have similar conversations.*

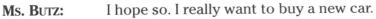

1. fix up my house
   $10,000
   at a hardware store

2. pay my bills
   $7,000
   at the airport

3. open a restaurant
   $25,000
   at McDonald's

4. take a vacation
   $2,000
   at the post office

5. buy a sailboat
   $12,000
   at the Regal Hotel

6. pay for my daughter's
   education
   $16,000
   at Nick's Garage

FREE RESPONSE • *Do you need to borrow money? What for?*

Listen and practice.

MR. PENFIELD: Miss Hackey, it's so nice of you to give me this interview.

MISS HACKEY: My pleasure.

MR. PENFIELD: Everyone's dying to hear about your new movie. Is it a romance?

MISS HACKEY: No, it's a drama. I play the part of a young woman who fights to save the family business.

MR. PENFIELD: What's the name of the movie?

MISS HACKEY: *That's My Business.*

MR. PENFIELD: Come on, you can tell me.

MISS HACKEY: I just told you, *That's My Business.*

MR. PENFIELD: Oh, I get it. *That's My Business* is the name of the movie.

MISS HACKEY: That's right. Would you like to see some stills of the movie?

MR. PENFIELD: I'd love to.

MISS HACKEY: OK, the first picture shows me with my father at the balloon factory. He's the president of the company.

MR. PENFIELD: What's happening in the second picture?

MISS HACKEY: He's having an argument with the manager of the loan company. My father has to repay the loan in five days or lose his business.

MR. PENFIELD: Does he have the money?

MISS HACKEY: No, and he's very worried. See, he's having a heart attack in the next picture.

MR. PENFIELD: The poor man.

MISS HACKEY: It's a desperate situation. Somehow I have to find the money to save the company—and my father's life.

MR. PENFIELD: What a story! How does it end?

MISS HACKEY: I can't tell you. You have to see the movie.

DIALOGUE QUESTIONS

1. What's the name of Miss Hackey's new movie?
2. What part does Miss Hackey play?
3. What kind of company does her father own?
4. Why is he worried?
5. What does Miss Hackey have to do?
6. How do you think the story ends?

CLASS ACTIVITY • *What's happening in these movie scenes? What do you think the characters are saying?*

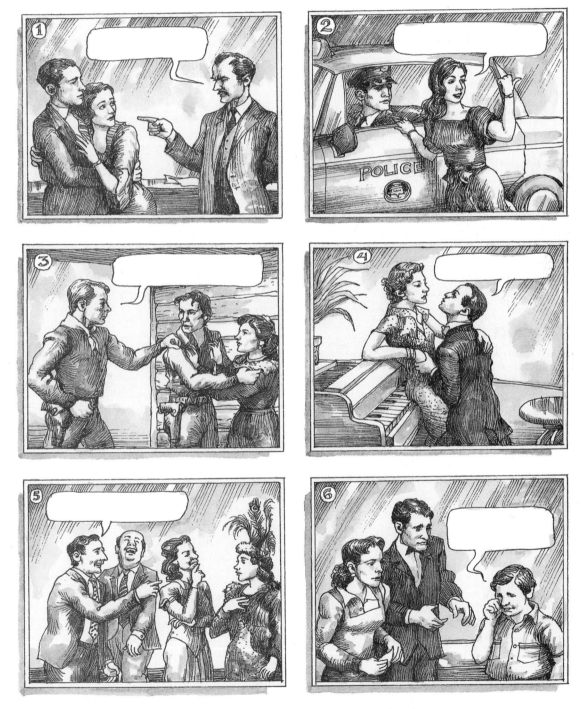

ROLE PLAY • *Choose one of these scenes and make up a conversation. Act out the scene before the class.*

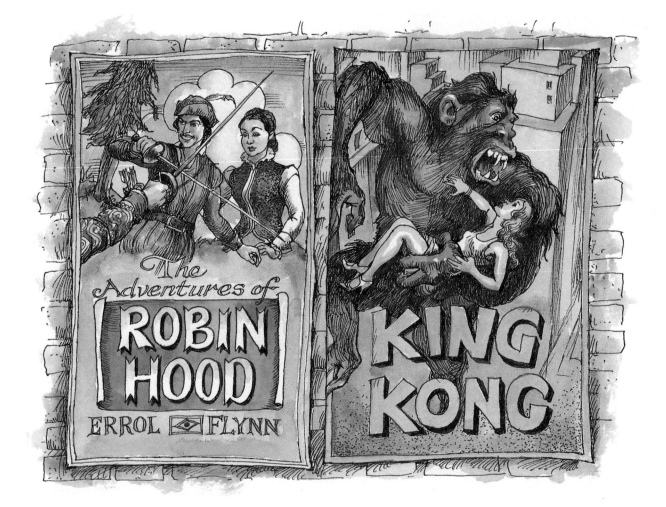

TALKING ABOUT MOVIES

1. What kind of movies do you like?
2. Do you have a favorite actor?
3. Who's your favorite actress?
4. What's your favorite movie?
5. What is the story about?
6 Who are the main characters?
7. What's your favorite scene in the movie?
8. How does the story end?
9. Are there any good movies playing now?

GROUP WORK • *Talk about movies with other students in your class.*

COMPOSITION • *Write about your favorite movie.*

GRAMMAR SUMMARY

PRESENT CONTINUOUS FOR FUTURE
Affirmative

They're	arriving on Monday. staying at the Wickam Hotel. leaving on Thursday.

Negative

They aren't	arriving on Monday. staying at the Wickam Hotel. leaving on Thursday.

Interrogative

Are they	arriving on Monday? staying at the Wickam Hotel? leaving on Thursday?

Short Answers

Yes, they are.	No, they aren't.

Compounds of SOME and ANY

They're	talking to	someone.
	buying	something.
	going	somewhere.

Questions with WHO, WHAT, and WHERE

Who		talking to?
What	are they	buying?
Where		going?

Interrogative

Are they	talking to	anyone?
	buying	anything?
	going	anywhere?

Negative

They aren't	talking to	anyone.
	buying	anything.
	going	anywhere.

MUST

He	has a nice girlfriend. can discuss anything.	He	must be	happy. intelligent.

They	play tennis every day. often go to the library.	They	must	like tennis. read a lot.

Chapter

3

TOPICS
Shopping
Occupations
Flattery

GRAMMAR
Too/enough
Both/neither/all/none
"Which (one) . . . ?"

FUNCTIONS
Identifying
Asking for and giving information
Communicating with gestures
Complimenting

1. Talk about the pictures.
2. Listen to the stories.
3. Answer the story questions.

READING

1 Mrs. Golo is having lunch at the Wickam Restaurant. She doesn't think it's a very good place to eat. The waiter brought her too many potatoes and not enough meat. And her coffee is too hot to drink. Mrs. Golo is saying something to the waiter, but he can't hear anything. The music in the restaurant is too loud.

1. Where is Mrs. Golo having lunch?
2. Does she think it's a good place to eat?
3. Did the waiter bring her enough potatoes?
4. What about meat?
5. Why can't Mrs. Golo drink her coffee?
6. Is she saying something to the waiter?
7. Why can't he hear her?

2 Johnnie is in the Wickam Department Store. He's trying on a new suit. He's unhappy because it doesn't fit him. The jacket is too small and the pants aren't long enough. Johnnie would like to buy his clothes at a more fashionable place, like the Continental Men's Shop. But it's expensive there and Johnnie doesn't have enough money this month.

1. Where's Johnnie?
2. What's he trying on?
3. Why is he unhappy?
4. Is the jacket the right size for Johnnie?
5. What about the pants?
6. Where would Johnnie like to buy his clothes?
7. Why doesn't he go to the Continental Men's Shop?

TOO AND ENOUGH	
The jacket is too small.	It isn't big enough.
_____ short.	_____ long _____.
_____ dark.	_____ light _____.
_____ old-fashioned.	_____ fashionable _____.

PRACTICE • *Make sentences with **too** + adjective.*

That suit isn't big enough for Johnnie.
It's too small.

Sam doesn't have enough time to go to the movies.
He's too busy.

1. Jimmy isn't old enough to drive a car.
2. Albert isn't tall enough to play basketball.
3. Linda isn't strong enough to lift those boxes.
4. Peter's car isn't big enough for five people.
5. Jack doesn't have enough money to buy a new car.
6. He doesn't have enough energy to clean his apartment.
7. Mr. Bascomb doesn't have enough time to play the piano.
8. It isn't hot enough to go to the beach.
9. That coat isn't heavy enough to wear in winter.

Listen and practice.

JENNY: Are you trying to pick some oranges, Marty?

MARTY: I can't reach them, Jenny. I'm not tall enough.

JENNY: It isn't worth it. They look too green.

MARTY: You're right. They probably aren't ripe enough to eat.

JENNY: Why don't you buy some oranges at the market?

MARTY: I don't have any money.

JENNY: I've got a dollar. Is that enough?

MARTY: That's enough to buy a whole bag of oranges. Let's go.

• *Ask and answer questions using* **too** *and* **enough.**

1. **A: Why can't Marty pick the oranges?**
   B: He isn't tall enough.
   OR **He's too short.**

2. **A: Why can't Johnnie lift the chair?**
   B: He isn't strong enough.
   OR **The chair is too heavy for him.**

3. Why isn't Albert enjoying the party?

4. Why can't Jimmy drink beer?

5. Why doesn't Jack cut the grass?

6. Why can't Fred hear Barney?

7. Why doesn't Mrs. Golo like her dinner?

8. Why doesn't Johnnie like his jacket?

Listen and repeat.

Both of these men are strong.
Neither of them is weak.

Both of these women are young.
Neither of them is old.

All of these bottles are empty.
None of them are full.

All of these watches are expensive.
None of them are cheap.

PRACTICE • *Make two sentences for each picture using **all, none, both,** and **neither.***

1. men/sick/well
   All of these men are sick.
   None of them are well.

2. girls/sad/happy
   Neither of these girls is sad.
   Both of them are happy.

3. boys/fat/thin

4. women/tall/short

5. glasses/full/empty

6. cameras/cheap/expensive

7. shoes/clean/dirty

8. guns/old/new

9. men/rich/poor

10. women/thin/fat

Listen and practice.

ALBERT: Hello, Mrs. Brown. Where's Linda?

MRS. BROWN: She went to the museum.

ALBERT: Which one did she go to?

MRS. BROWN: She went to the Art Museum.

ALBERT: Did she walk?

MRS. BROWN: No, she took the bus.

ALBERT: Which bus did she take?

MRS. BROWN: The red one, number thirty-six.

SAM BROWN: Can you show me the hat on the shelf?

SALESMAN: Which hat, the brown one or the gray one?

SAM BROWN: The brown one.

SALESMAN: Here, try it on. Let's see how it looks.

SAM BROWN: Hmm. It's not exactly the right size.

SALESMAN: Let's try the other one.

1. Men's Hats

CUSTOMER: Can you show me the *hat*, please?

SALESPERSON: Which *hat*, the *brown* one or the *gray* one?

CUSTOMER: The *brown* one.

2. Dresses

3. Handbags *large & small*

4. umbrellas

5. Watches — $250 — $30

6. Dolls

7. ★CARS★ — NEW — USED

Peter is at the bookshop. He wants to get Maria a book for her birthday. The other day Nancy recommended a book called *The Voyage of the Cat.* But Peter was in a hurry, and now he can't remember anything she told him. One of the salespeople is trying to help Peter.

"Is it some kind of historical book?" she asks.

"No, it isn't anything historical," he says. "It's a new book by someone with a funny name."

"Well," she says, "all the new books are on this shelf. Is it one of these?"

"No, it's none of those. But now I remember. The author's name is Ken Killuga."

"Of course," says the saleswoman. "We have two books by Ken Killuga in the window. Which one do you want?"

"I still can't remember."

"Why don't you take both of them?"

"I can't," says Peter. "They're too expensive, and perhaps neither of them is the one she wants."

"Whatever you say," says the saleswoman. She smiles at Peter. "I think your girlfriend is very lucky. She must be intelligent, too."

"You're right, she is. But how did you know?"

"It's obvious. She has such a pleasant, good-looking boyfriend."

"Well, thank you," says Peter, smiling happily. "On second thought, I'll take both books."

STORY QUESTIONS

1. Does Peter want to get a book for his mother?
2. What's the name of the book Nancy recommended? Who's the author?
3. How many of Ken Killuga's books are in the window?
4. Why doesn't Peter take both of them right away?
5. Why does the saleswoman think Peter's girlfriend is lucky?
6. Why does Peter decide to take both books?
7. Do you think the saleswoman is smart? Why?

PAIR WORK • *Ask and answer questions.*

A: **Where can I get a doll?**
B: **At the toy store.**

A: **Is there a toy store nearby?**
B: **Yes, there's one on Clark Street.**

1. some roses
2. a chocolate cake
3. some cologne
4. some pens
5. a ball
6. a radio
7. some perfume
8. some cookies
9. a model train
10. some speakers
11. some envelopes
12. some daisies

Listen and practice.

PAIR WORK • *Have similar conversations.*

1. bakery
2. stationery store
3. stereo center
4. toy store
5. flower shop
6. beauty supply
7. market
8. department store
9. drug store

CONVERSATION

Listen and practice.

TINO: What do you have there, Peter?

PETER: Some books. I got them for Maria.

TINO: Were they expensive?

PETER: Yes. I paid forty dollars for them.

TINO: Where did you get them?

PETER: At Johnnie's Bookstore.

PAIR WORK • *Have similar conversations.*

A: What do you have there, _____?

B: _____. I got it/them for _____.

A: _____ expensive?

B: Yes I paid _____ for it/them.

  OR No. I only paid _____ for it/them.

A: Where did you get _____?

B: At _____.

1. Barney Field—taxi driver

I drive a taxi in Wickam City. I grew up here, so I know the streets of this town like I know the back of my hand. I try to be friendly with all of my customers, but sometimes I have difficult passengers. When I'm stressed out, I play soft music on the radio. It helps me to relax.

2. Sara "Mom" Hawkins—cafe owner

I own a cafe called "Mom's." We're located in the center of town, and we have a lot of customers. Folks like to eat here because we serve good food in a friendly atmosphere. I do most of the cooking, so I'm here all the time. I guess you could say I'm married to this place.

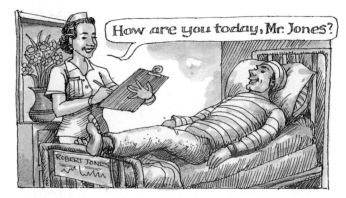

3. Luisa Santana—nurse

I work as a general nurse at Frampton Hospital. I take care of all kinds of patients. I became a nurse because I like to help people who are in pain. I like to see people leave the hospital with a smile on their face. I love it when my patients say, "Thank you. You really helped me."

4. Elmer Coggins—farmer

I have a small farm in California. I grow corn and raise pigs and chickens. It's a hard life. I work all day from sun up to sun down, and I hardly ever take a rest. But I enjoy being a farmer. It makes me feel good to produce food for people who live in the city.

PAIR WORK • *Tell what you think of each person's job. Use the adjectives in the box.*

A: **What do you think of Barney's job?**

B: **I think he has an easy job. Anyone can drive a taxi.**

A: **I agree.**   OR   **I disagree. I think . . .**

good	difficult
interesting	wonderful
boring	exciting
terrible	dangerous
easy	stressful
hard	relaxing

GROUP WORK • *Talk about the people in the pictures. What are they doing? Do you think they have interesting jobs? Why or why not?*

1. Suzi Suzuki—reporter

2. Tino Martinoli—waiter

3. Anne Jones—secretary

4. Richard Poole—teacher

5. Ula Hackey—actress

6. Grover Muldoon—
   police officer

COMPOSITION • *Imagine you are one of the people above. Write a paragraph describing your job. Tell what you like or don't like about your job and explain why. Or, if you wish, write about your real job.*

PAIR WORK • *Interview your partner about his or her job. Ask these questions and make up your own questions.*

- What do you do for a living?
- Where do you work?
- What hours do you work?
- Do you like your boss? Why?

- Do you meet interesting people on the job?
- What is hard about your job?
- What do you like about your job?
- What other work would you like to do? Why?

GESTURES

WRITTEN EXERCISE • *The people in these pictures are talking with their hands. Can you tell what they are saying? Write an appropriate sentence for each one. There can be more than one appropriate sentence for each picture.*

FREE RESPONSE

1. Do these gestures mean the same thing all over the world?
2. What gestures do people in your country make when they greet each other?
3. How do you say something is "no good" with a gesture?
4. How do you say "I love you" with a gesture?
5. What are some other things people say with their hands?
6. How can you say "I'm hungry" with your hands?
7. How can you get the attention of a waiter without speaking?
8. Do you use your hands when you talk? How?

GROUP WORK • *Take turns making gestures. The others in your group try to guess what you are saying with your hands.*

The salesman is giving Mrs. Bascomb a nice compliment. He's flattering her.

TALKING ABOUT FLATTERY

1. Why do people use flattery?
2. Do you think flattery is OK? Why or why not?
3. What are some compliments that you give your friends?
4. What are some compliments that you get from other people?
5. Give a compliment to the person sitting next to you.

good service

bad service

TALKING ABOUT SHOPPING

1. Do you like to shop?
2. What are some clothes you need to buy?
3. Where is a good place to shop for clothes?
4. Is the service good in most stores?
5. Are most salespeople courteous and helpful?

COMPOSITION • *Write about a good place to go shopping. Why do you shop there?*

ENOUGH

That dress isn't | big
long | enough for Linda.
pretty

TOO

It's too | small.
short.
plain.

ENOUGH

Mrs. Golo doesn't have enough | time to go to the library.
energy to clean the house.
strength to lift that table.

TOO

She's too | busy (to go to the library).
tired (to clean the house).
weak (to lift that table).

ALL/NONE

| All
None | of those men are intelligent. |

ALL

They're all intelligent.

BOTH/NEITHER

| Both
Neither | of these books | are
is | expensive. |

BOTH

They're both expensive.

Question with WHICH

| He's going to the library. | Which | library
one | is he going to? |

Review Chapter

TOPICS
Renting an apartment
Free time

GRAMMAR
Review

FUNCTIONS
Inquiring about an apartment for rent
Describing personal traits
Giving reasons and explanations
Expressing feelings/emotions
Making complaints

Johnnie Wilson is very unhappy these days. He shares a small apartment with his Uncle Ed, and Ed is a very difficult person to live with. He has a lot of bad habits. Ed doesn't like to take a bath or change his clothes, and he never cleans up the apartment. He leaves his dirty dishes in the sink and his empty soda cans in the living room, and he never washes his dog, Brutus.

When Johnnie comes home, he can't relax because Ed is always watching TV and playing his bongos. He can't sit in his favorite chair because Brutus is always there. And Johnnie can hardly breathe because of Ed's cigar smoke, which is killing Johnnie's plants.

Johnnie has to pay the rent because Ed never has any money—he's always broke. Ed is unemployed, and he says he can't find a job. But the truth is, he doesn't want to work. Ed has an easy, comfortable life, and that's the way he likes it.

Of course, Johnnie doesn't like the situation. But what can he do about it? Whenever he complains, Ed either ignores him or leaves the room. And Johnnie hates to be alone in the same room with Brutus. He knows Brutus has sharp teeth and a bad attitude.

At the moment, Johnnie is looking for some food in the refrigerator. He's very hungry after working hard all day. Unfortunately, Ed and Brutus got there first.

"You two are really disgusting!" cries Johnnie. "You took all the food and didn't leave anything for me."

"Don't worry," says Ed, his mouth full of spaghetti. "The market's still open. You can go there and buy more."

"No more!" says Johnnie, angrily. "I'm not buying any more food for you and that animal. From now on, you can pay for your own food—and the rent. I'm moving out!"

"You can't do that," says Ed, wiping his fingers on his T-shirt.

"Oh, no?" says Johnnie. "Watch me."

Ed and Brutus look very surprised as Johnnie goes to his room, packs his suitcase, and walks out of the apartment.

STORY QUESTIONS

1. Who does Johnnie live with?
2. What are some of Ed's bad habits?
3. Why can't Johnnie relax when he comes home?
4. Why can't he sit in his favorite chair?
5. Why are Johnnie's plants dying?
6. Why does Johnnie have to pay the rent?
7. Why doesn't Ed work?
8. What happens when Johnnie complains to Ed?
9. Why is Johnnie afraid of Brutus?
10. What's Johnnie doing in the kitchen?
11. Why is the refrigerator empty?
12. What does Johnnie decide to do about the situation?

FREE RESPONSE

1. Do you have a roommate? Describe him or her.
2. Are you an easy person to live with?
3. Do you have any bad habits?
4. What are your good points?
5. Do you know anyone like Ed?
6. What are your neighbors like?
7. Do you ever have problems with your neighbors?
8. Do you ever complain? What things make you angry?

Listen and practice.

JOHNNIE:	Hello, can I speak to Miss Blake, please?
BLOSSOM:	This is Blossom Blake.
JOHNNIE:	Are you the manager of the Sherwood Oaks Apartments?
BLOSSOM:	That's right. What can I do for you?
JOHNNIE:	I'm calling about the apartment you have for rent. Is it still available?
BLOSSOM:	Yes, it is. Why don't you come and take a look at it?
JOHNNIE:	Okay, but I want to ask you some questions first.
BLOSSOM:	Sure, what do you want to know?
JOHNNIE:	Your ad says the rent is six hundred dollars a month. Does that include utilities?
BLOSSOM:	The water is included. But you pay for gas and electricity.
JOHNNIE:	Is the apartment furnished?
BLOSSOM:	Yes. There's a bed, sofa, dining table, and two chairs.
JOHNNIE:	I see. Can you tell me anything about the tenants? What are they like?
BLOSSOM:	Oh, all the tenants are nice, friendly people.
JOHNNIE:	That's good. Does the apartment have a view?
BLOSSOM:	Yes. There's an interesting view from the bedroom window.
JOHNNIE:	Great. When can I see the apartment?
BLOSSOM:	I'm here all day. Come any time you like.
JOHNNIE:	I'm coming now.
BLOSSOM:	Wait a minute. What's your name?
JOHNNIE:	Johnnie Wilson.
BLOSSOM:	See you soon, Johnnie. Bye-bye.

DIALOGUE QUESTIONS

1. Who is Blossom Blake?
2. Why is Johnnie calling her?
3. How did he find out about the apartment?
4. How much is the rent?
5. Are the utilities included?
6. What kind of furniture does the apartment have?
7. What are the tenants like?
8. When is Johnnie going to see the apartment?
9. What's the address of the Sherwood Oaks Apartments?

*****************************CLASSIFIED ADS*****************************

1	WICKAM CITY $435 Single unfurn. New paint, utils. incl., pool, prkg. Xlnt loc. Call Manager 555-3528	WICKAM CITY $675 Attractive 2 Bdrm. Small, clean, quiet bldg. No pets. 555-2285 after 5 pm	4
2	WICKAM CITY $525 Nice 1 Bdrm. stv/frig, A/C, balc. great view! Children OK! Call 555-2186	WICKAM CITY $700 2 bdrm., 2 ba. Utils. free, new carpet, stv/frig. Near shops & transp. 555-5097	5
3	WICKAM CITY $450 1 Bdrm. furn. laundry, prkg. Good neighborhood. Close to shopping & transp. 555-3751	WICKAM CITY $1,200 3 Bdrm. hse. Large rooms, fireplace, view, grdn. 2-car garage. 555-2536 9–5 pm	6

ABBREVIATIONS

A/C	= air conditioning	cpt.	= carpet	prkg.	= parking
apt.	= apartment	frig.	= refrigerator	stv.	= stove
ba.	= bathroom	furn.	= furnished	transp.	= transportation
balc.	= balcony	grdn.	= garden	unfurn.	= unfurnished
bdrm.	= bedroom	hse.	= house	utils. incl.	= utilities included
bldg.	= building	lndry.	= laundry	xlnt. loc.	= excellent location

PRACTICE • *Study the abbreviated words and then describe the apartments in the classified ads.*

> It's a single, unfurnished apartment. It has new paint and the utilities are included. . . .

PAIR WORK • *Have a conversation like the one on page 56. Student A is looking for an apartment and Student B is the manager. You can use the classified ads above or make up your own.*

Student A: Phone the manager and
(1) ask him or her to describe the apartment
(2) ask for any more information you need: utilities? parking? other tenants? quiet?
(3) decide to go and see the apartment
(4) ask how to get there

Student B: Answer the phone and
(1) describe the apartment
(2) answer any more questions about the apartment (say good things about it)
(3) ask if he or she is coming to see it
(4) tell him or her how to get there

GROUP WORK • *What things are important to you when you look for an apartment? Make a list of the five most important things.*

Five minutes after his telephone conversation with Miss Blake, Johnnie arrives at the Sherwood Oaks Apartments. He goes up to the manager's apartment and knocks on the door.

"I'm coming," yells Miss Blake from inside. The door opens and Blossom Blake appears. She is a thin, middle-aged woman with straight brown hair. "You must be Johnnie Wilson."

Johnnie nods his head affirmatively.

"You sure got here fast," says Blossom.

"I have to find an apartment right away," says Johnnie. "I don't have any place to stay."

"Well, this is your lucky day," says Blossom. "I have the perfect apartment for you. Come with me."

Johnnie follows Blossom down the long hallway that leads to the back of the building. He sees three men at the end of the hallway. They're sitting in a circle playing cards. Blossom frowns.

"I thought I told you boys not to play in the building."

"Sorry, Blossom," says Curly, the leader of the gang. "We forgot."

"Boys, this is Johnnie Wilson. He's here to look at your old apartment."

"Oh, you're going to like it," says Curly. "It's a cool apartment."

"There it is," says Blossom, pointing to apartment thirteen. She takes out her key and opens the door. "After you, Johnnie."

Johnnie enters the apartment. It's dark inside, with just one small light-bulb hanging from the ceiling. He looks around the room and his mouth drops open. Everything in the apartment is in bad condition; the furniture is broken, the walls have cracks, and the roof leaks. Johnnie looks down and sees a large bucket on the floor. It's full of water.

"Don't worry," says Blossom. "We're going to repair the roof."

"When?" asks Johnnie.

"Soon. Maybe this summer. Anyway, it's not a big problem."

"What?" says Johnnie.

Blossom smiles. "Look," she says, "the water only drips during the rainy season, and it only drips in the living room. The rest of the apartment is dry."

"I'm glad to know that," says Johnnie. "Can I see the bedroom now?"

"Yes, of course," says Blossom. "Come with me." She leads Johnnie into the bedroom.

"The bed doesn't look very comfortable," says Johnnie.

"Well, it is a little soft," says Blossom. "But when you're tired, it doesn't make any difference."

"Why are the curtains closed?" asks Johnnie. "Are you trying to hide something?"

"Not at all," says Blossom. "Do you want to see the view?"

"Please," says Johnnie.

Blossom pulls back the curtains and Johnnie looks out the window. Across the street is a junkyard full of old, wrecked cars. Johnnie sees a big dog sitting on top of one of the cars. The dog looks like Brutus. Suddenly, Johnnie feels a sharp pain in his chest.

"Well, how do you like the apartment?" asks Blossom.

Johnnie is very polite. He doesn't like to criticize. "I don't think this is the right apartment for me," he says.

"Why not?"

"Well, six hundred dollars is a lot of money. I don't think I can afford to pay the rent."

"Why didn't you think of that before you came here?"

"Well, to be honest, this apartment isn't very good. In fact, it's terrible. I'm going to stay with my Uncle Ed. Good-bye."

"Wait a minute," says Blossom, looking very surprised. "Your uncle's name is Ed? Ed Wilson?"

"That's right. Why?"

Blossom sits down on the bed. "This is unbelievable," she says. "Ed Wilson is my old boyfriend. We were high school sweethearts."

"Oh, no, you're mistaken," says Johnnie. "It must be a different Ed Wilson. You see, my Uncle Ed is a bum. He never does anything."

"That's him!" cries Blossom, happily. "And you're his nephew. Isn't it a small world?" Johnnie tries to leave, but Blossom stops him. "You can't leave without giving me your address," she says, standing between Johnnie and the door. Johnnie looks very uncomfortable. "Come on, you can tell me," says Blossom, smiling sweetly.

"Oh, all right," says Johnnie. "It's one eighty-five Bond Street."

Blossom claps her hands. "I'm so happy," she says. "I can't wait to see Eddie again. I'm going to come and visit you."

"Oh, wonderful," says Johnnie, walking out of the apartment. "This sure is my lucky day."

STORY QUESTIONS

1. When did Johnnie arrive at the Sherwood Oaks Apartments?
2. What is Blossom Blake like? Describe her.
3. Why is Johnnie in a hurry to find an apartment?
4. Why does Blossom tell Johnnie, "This is your lucky day"?
5. What does Johnnie see at the end of the hallway?
6. What are the three men doing?
7. Why is Blossom unhappy?
8. Who is the leader of the gang?
9. What does Curly say about their old apartment?
10. What is apartment thirteen really like? What's wrong with it?
11. Why isn't Blossom worried about the roof?
12. What does Johnnie see when he looks out the bedroom window?
13. What reason does Johnnie give for not taking the apartment?
14 What is the real reason he doesn't want the apartment?
15. Why is Blossom so happy when she finds out that Johnnie's uncle is Ed Wilson?
16. What happens when Johnnie tries to leave the apartment?
17. Why does Blossom want Johnnie's address?
18. Do you believe Johnnie when he says, "This sure is my lucky day"?

WRITTEN EXERCISE • *What is your opinion of Ed, Brutus, and Johnnie? Describe them using some of the adjectives from this list. Can you think of any other adjectives to describe them?*

polite ≠ rude	smart ≠ dumb	weak ≠ strong
generous ≠ selfish	happy ≠ unhappy	timid ≠ aggressive
loud ≠ quiet	harmless ≠ dangerous	neat ≠ sloppy
lazy ≠ hardworking	pleasant ≠ disgusting	mean ≠ gentle

Ed

selfish

Brutus

mean

Johnnie

timid

COMPOSITION • *A week later, Blossom goes to visit Ed and Johnnie. Ed is very happy to see Blossom. He asks her for a date and she accepts. Write a short composition about their date. Where do they go? What do you think happens?*

FREE RESPONSE

1. Is it easy or difficult to find an apartment in your city?
2. Describe your house or apartment.
3. What kind of furniture do you have in your living room?
4. Do you have a nice view? What can you see from your living room window?
5. Do you live near shopping and transportation? Are you in a good location?
6. Describe the street you live on. Is it wide or narrow? quiet or noisy?
7. Do you know most of your neighbors? How often do you talk with them?
8. What are your neighbors like? Are they friendly?
9. Do you like your neighbors? Why or why not?

PAIR WORK • *Ask and answer questions using these adverbs of frequency:* **always, often, usually, sometimes, seldom,** *and* **never.**

> take the bus
> A: **How often do you take the bus?**
> B: **I always take the bus.** OR **I seldom take the bus.**

1. drink coffee
2. make breakfast
3. walk to school
4. study at the library
5. talk about sports
6. listen to rock music
7. wear jeans
8. play cards
9. write letters
10. read the newspaper
11. watch TV
12. go to the movies

WRITTEN EXERCISE • *Add sentences that explain or give a reason for the first sentence.*

> Ed is a difficult person to live with. *He has a lot of bad habits.*
> OR *He's very selfish.*
> Can you loan me five dollars? *I'm broke.*
> OR *I need to buy some gas.*

1. I can't go to the movies with you tonight. _____

2. Anne doesn't like her job. _____

3. Mr. and Mrs. Golo are saving their money. _____

4. Barbara and Tino want to visit Paris. _____

5. We always eat at Mom's Cafe. _____

6. We like our neighbors. _____

7. My sister is very happy today. _____

8. I'm mad at my brother. _____

9. I can't talk to you now. _____

10. I'm tired. _____

Listen and repeat.

Consider the different ways you can express your feelings.

I think it's beautiful.	It depresses me.	It makes me sad.
_____ exciting.	_ worries _____.	_____ happy.
_____ awful.	_ scares _____.	_____ angry.
_____ nice.	_ bores _____.	_____ nervous.

GROUP WORK • *How do you feel about the pictures below? Discuss them with other students.*

WRITTEN EXERCISE 1 • *Complete the sentences using the affirmative or negative form of* **have to** + *verb.*

Our team (win) *has to win* the football game. It's very important.

There's plenty of time, so we (hurry) *don't have to hurry* .

1. Gloria's car is at the garage. She (take) _____ the bus to work.

2. She (get up) _____ early. Her job doesn't start until noon.

3. You (attend) _____ the meeting. It isn't necessary.

4. I (go) _____ now. My sister is waiting for me.

5. Jack has an easy life. He (work) _____ very hard.

6. His refrigerator is empty. He (go) _____ to the market.

7. You (make) _____ dinner. We can go to a restaurant.

8. We (stop) _____ at a gas station. There's hardly any gas in the tank.

9. Maria (cut) _____ her hair. It's getting too long.

10. She (use) _____ make up. She looks good without it.

11. I (clean up) _____ my apartment. It looks terrible.

12. You (help) _____ me. I can do it alone.

WRITTEN EXERCISE 2 • *Complete the sentences using* **a lot of, much, many, a few,** *and* **a little.**

Maria likes her coffee with a lot of cream but only *a little* sugar.

There aren't *many* cups on the shelf.

1. Mr. Bascomb is a busy man. He doesn't have _____ free time.

2. He works hard and makes _____ money.

3. He knows a lot of people, but he doesn't have _____ good friends.

4. There are only _____ people at the Martinoli Restaurant today.

5. Anne isn't very hungry. She's only having _____ soup for lunch.

6. Tino is very athletic and plays _____ sports.

7. How _____ sports can Barbara play?

8. Mrs. Golo has a lot of envelopes, but she has only _____ stamps.

9. How _____ paper does she have?

PICTURE PRACTICE• *What is Barbara doing in these pictures? How long does it take her to get ready for a date?*

PAIR WORK • *Ask and answer questions.*

> walk to the market
> A: **How long does it take you to walk to the market?**
> B: **It takes me about five minutes.**

1. take a shower
2. wash your hair
3. get dressed
4. eat breakfast
5. make the bed
6. get ready for a date
7. walk to the post office
8. read the newspaper
9. write a letter
10. make a cup of coffee
11. brush your teeth
12. wash your clothes

WRITTEN EXERCISE • *Complete the following sentences using these prepositions:* ***for, of, from, with, in,*** *and* ***to.***

> My sister lives *with* her husband *in* in New York.

1. Barbara is getting ready _____ her date _____ Tino.

2. He invited her _____ a movie.

3. Anne lives a long distance _____ her job.

4. She usually takes the bus _____ work.

5. The manager _____ our apartment building is very friendly.

6. He's nice _____ everyone.

7. Otis bought an expensive present _____ Gloria.

8. It was a bottle _____ perfume _____ France.

9. We're taking a trip _____ Mexico _____ June.

10. Mexico is famous _____ its beautiful beaches.

11. Can you help me _____ my homework?

12. I don't understand some _____ the exercises _____ this chapter.

PAIR WORK • *Ask and answer questions. Use the present, past, and future tenses.*

tomorrow	last weekend
A: **What are you going to do tomorrow?**	A: **What did you do last weekend?**
B: **I'm going to see a movie.**	B: **I went to the beach.**

1. last night
2. this weekend
3. every morning
4. right now
5. after this class
6. yesterday
7. tonight
8. on weekends
9. last Sunday
10. today
11. in your free time
12. this Saturday

WRITTEN EXERCISE • *Complete the sentences using adjectives. There can be more than one possible answer.*

Barney told a _funny_ story and everyone laughed.

1. Jenny is very _____. She always says "please" and "thank you."

2. Anyone can ride a bicycle. It's _____.

3. Sam is _____ because he worked hard all day.

4. Ed is _____. He never does any work.

5. Someone drank all the soda. The bottle is _____.

6. We have to hurry. We're _____ for the concert.

7. The concert is _____. We don't have to pay.

8. Maria is _____ because she can't find her car keys.

9. The theater is only a _____ distance from here. We can walk.

10. There's no danger. The streets are _____ in this neighborhood.

FREE RESPONSE

1. Where did you go after class yesterday? What did you do?
2. What did you have for dinner last night?
3. Do you eat between meals? What is your favorite snack?
4. Are you a good cook? What can you make?
5. Do you like to stay up late and watch TV or read?
6. Did you sleep well last night? How many hours did you sleep?
7. What time did you wake up this morning? What did you have for breakfast?
8. Do you like to go for walks? Where are some good places to take a walk?
9. Are you busy most of the time? What keeps you busy?
10. What are some things you have to do this week?
11. Do you have enough time for everything? work? play? family? friends?
12. What are your plans for this weekend?

🎧 *Listen and read.*

STORY QUESTIONS

1. What does George like to watch on TV?
2. What happened that made George unhappy?
3. What is your opinion of George? Is he a "couch potato"?
4. Do you think people watch too much TV?
5. How often do you watch TV? What programs do you watch?
6. Do you like to read books? What kind?
7. Can you learn more from books or television?
8. What do you like to do with your free time?

ROLE PLAY

Student A plays Johnnie. Student B plays Ed.
Situation: Johnnie complains about Ed's bad habits. Ed tells Johnnie that he isn't perfect
either. Read and practice the complaints and responses listed below. Then close your
books and create a conversation.

Possible complaints:

You leave your things all over the place.
You make a mess in the kitchen.
You never wash the dishes.
You never go to the market.
I have to pay for everything.
You're always on the phone.
You never think of me.
You don't do your share.

Possible responses:

So what?
That's not true.
I don't feel like it.
I'm too busy.
That's what you think.
What about you?
That's too bad.
You complain too much.

TALKING ABOUT SARCASM

When Johnnie says to Blossom, "This sure is my lucky day," he doesn't really
mean it. This is an example of sarcasm: a person says one thing when he or
she means exactly the opposite. We know that Johnnie doesn't feel lucky at
all. He feels very unlucky because everything went wrong. People often use
sarcasm when they are upset about something or they want to be funny.
Here are some more examples of sarcasm:

You lose your keys and say, "That was smart of me."
You say to someone who is lazy, "Don't work too hard."

1. Can you give an example of sarcasm?
2. Do you think it's OK to use sarcasm?
3. Do you always know when someone is being sarcastic?
4. Do people often use sarcasm in your country?
5. Do you ever use sarcasm?

1. Sam is very popular.

   He has _____ friends.
   A. much   C. a few
   B. a lot of   D. any

2. Mr. Bascomb is a busy man.

   He doesn't have _____ free time.
   A. much   C. some
   B. many   D. no

3. We need some matches. We don't have

   _____.

   A. much   C. any
   B. some   D. none

4. Barbara likes her coffee with _____ sugar.
   A. much   C. a few
   B. many   D. a little

5. Hurry up! The show starts in _____ minutes.
   A. many   C. a few
   B. much   D. a lot of

6. There aren't _____ people in the theater.
   A. many   C. some
   B. much   D. no

7. Peter enjoys his work _____ it's interesting.
   A. although   C. so
   B. because   D. but

8. It was warm and sunny yesterday,

   _____ I went to the beach.
   A. although   C. so
   B. because   D. but

9. Barney borrowed some money

   _____ the bank last month.
   A. for   C. to
   B. of   D. from

10. He thanked Mr. Bascomb _____ his help.
    A. for   C. to
    B. of   D. from

11. We're taking our vacation _____ August.
    A. for   C. on
    B. at   D. in

12. Nancy is going _____ France next year.
    A. in   C. at
    B. to   D. on

13. Johnnie lives _____ Bond Street.
    A. at   C. on
    B. in   D. to

14. I usually have lunch _____ one o'clock.
    A. at   C. on
    B. in   D. from

15. Those aren't your magazines.

    Don't take _____.
    A. they   C. this
    B. them   D. that

16. Here's my phone number. You can call

    _____ at home.
    A. I   C. mine
    B. my   D. me

17. Where's your brother? I have to talk

    with _____.
    A. he   C. him
    B. her   D. them

18. _____ did Mr. Wankie sell his car?
    Because he needed the money.
    A. How   C. Where
    B. Why   D. When

19. _____ did Linda go home?
    At three o'clock.
    A. When   C. Why
    B. Where   D. How

20. _____ does Mrs. Hamby work?
    At the post office.
    A. How   C. When
    B. Why   D. Where

21. _____ pencil do you want, the red one or the blue one?
   A. Whose   C. Which
   B. What   D. Who's

22. Jane doesn't have _____ in her handbag.
   A. something   C. nothing
   B. anything   D. none

23. Our club is having a big party Saturday night. _____ is going.
   A. Someone   C. Everyone
   B. Anyone   D. Every person

24. Jimmy can't go _____ this afternoon. He has to do his homework.
   A. nowhere   C. somewhere
   B. everywhere D. anywhere

25. I like Jimmy and Linda. They're _____ good friends of mine.
   A. both   C. either
   B. all   D. neither

26. Ed ate all the cookies. There are _____ left.
   A. nothing   C. some
   B. none   D. any

27. We all make mistakes. Nobody's _____.
   A. perfect   C. good
   B. wonderful   D. fine

28. People usually speak _____ in the library.
   A. quiet   C. soft
   B. loudly   D. softly

29. Mr. Bascomb can't see very _____ without his glasses.
   A. good   C. well
   B. perfect   D. fine

30. Put on your coat. It's _____ outside.
   A. hot   C. warm
   B. cold   D. sunny

31. I have to do _____ homework.
   A. my   C. mine
   B. me   D. many

32. The Golos are painting _____ kitchen.
   A. there   C. their
   B. they're D. theirs

33. We're taking the typewriter because it's _____.
   A. yours   C. our
   B. theirs   D. ours

34. Gloria says those envelopes are _____.
   A. her   C. our
   B. hers   D. your

35. Listen! Someone _____.
   A. come   C. is coming
   B. comes   D. are coming

36. The refrigerator is empty. We _____ go to the market.
   A. has to   C. like to
   B. have to   D. needs to

37. Where are the boys? They _____ in the park.
   A. play   C. is playing
   B. plays   D. are playing

38. I never _____ a hat.
   A. wear   C. am wearing
   B. wears   D. is wearing

39. Barney _____ to a movie yesterday.
   A. go   C. is going
   B. goes   D. went

40. Does Peter drive a sports car? Yes, he _____.
   A. do   C. drive
   B. does   D. drives

41. Did Maria work last Saturday?

    No, she _____.

    A. did   C. worked
    B. didn't   D. not work

42. You don't have much free time,

    _____?

    A. don't you   C. you do
    B. you don't   D. do you

43. It's a beautiful day, _____?

    A. it's not   C. isn't it
    B. it is   D. it isn't

44. Your apartment is close to everything.

    You live in a good _____.

    A. situation   C. location
    B. condition   D. station

45. Sam worked very hard. He must be

    _____.

    A. tired   C. polite
    B. weak   D. lazy

46. Anne has a lot of problems. _____

    A. Practice makes perfect.
    B. That nice of her.
    C. That sounds like fun.
    D. That's too bad.

47. She doesn't like to work for Mr. Bascomb.

    She thinks he's a bad _____.

    A. boss   C. employee
    B. owner   D. customer

48. The _____ for this apartment is
    three hundred dollars a month.

    A. price   C. bill
    B. rent   D. pay

49. Ed doesn't have any money. He's

    _____.

    A. broke   C. wrecked
    B. broken   D. middle-aged

50. London is the capital of England, isn't it?

    _____

    A. You're mistaken.
    B. It's a small world.
    C. That's right.
    D. Not at all.

Chapter

TOPICS
Clothes
Travel
Eating out
The future

GRAMMAR
Future with "will"
Shall (offers)
May (permission)
Would like to . . .

FUNCTIONS
Giving reasons and explanations
Making offers
Asking for permission
Asking for favors
Making suggestions
Making predictions
Ordering a meal in a restaurant

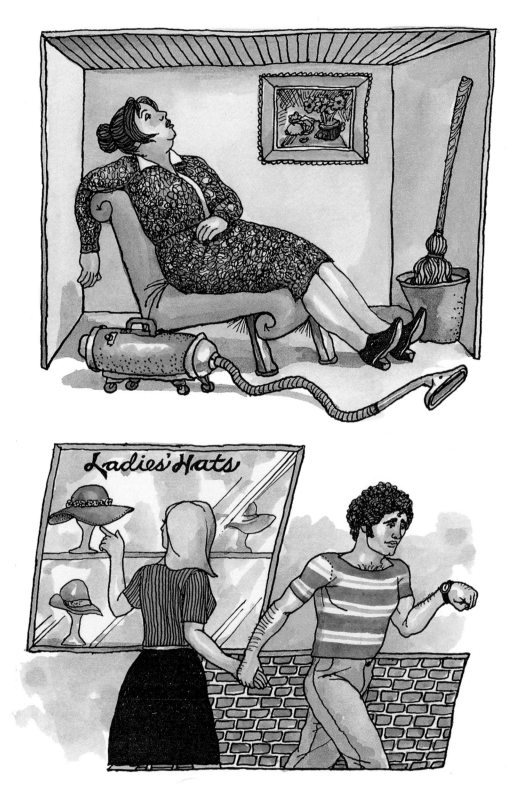

1. *Talk about the pictures.*
2. *Listen to the stories.*
3. *Answer the questions.*

READING

1 Mrs. Brown planned to go to the market today. She wanted to get some steak for dinner because it's on sale this week. However, she decided to stay home and clean the house. She'll go to the market tomorrow. At the moment, Mrs. Brown is resting. She's very tired after all the housework she did today.

1. Where did Mrs. Brown plan to go today?
2. Why did she want to get steak for dinner?
3. What did Mrs. Brown decide to do?
4. When will she go to the market?
5. What do you think she'll get?
6. What is Mrs. Brown doing at the moment?
7. Why is she tired?

2 Tino is very fond of Barbara and often buys her presents. However, this week he was very busy and didn't buy her anything. Perhaps he'll give her something next week. Right now Barbara and Tino are walking to the bus stop. Barbara wants to stop and look at some hats. But Tino is in a hurry. He's afraid they'll miss the bus.

1. Does Tino often buy presents for Barbara?
2. Did he buy her anything this week?
3. Why not?
4. Do you think he'll give her something next week?
5. What do you think he'll give her?
6. Where are Barbara and Tino going now?
7. Why is Tino in a hurry?

FUTURE WITH **WILL**: AFFIRMATIVE	
She'll go to the market tomorrow.	She will go to the market tomorrow.
He'll _____.	He will _____.
I'll _____.	I will _____.
You'll _____.	You will _____.
We'll _____.	We will _____.
They'll _____.	They will _____.

PRACTICE • *Make affirmative sentences with **will**.*

Mrs. Brown didn't go to the market today. (tomorrow)
She'll go to the market tomorrow.

1. Peter didn't call Maria last night. (tonight)
2. He didn't go to the office today. (tomorrow)
3. Linda didn't see Albert yesterday. (on Saturday)
4. They didn't have a party this week. (next week)
5. Jimmy didn't do his homework today. (tomorrow)
6. Mrs. Golo didn't make dinner last night. (tonight)
7. She didn't feed the cat yesterday. (today)
8. I didn't wash the car this week. (next week)
9. Nancy didn't visit Paris last March. (in June)

CONVERSATION

Listen and practice.

SALESWOMAN: May I help you?

BARBARA: Yes. Could you show me your *summer dresses,* please?

SALESWOMAN: I'll be happy to.

BARBARA: This one's very nice.

SALESWOMAN: It's on sale. It's only *thirty-nine dollars.*

BARBARA: Good. I think I'll get it.

PAIR WORK • *Have similar conversations.*

1. summer dresses
$39

2. sport coats
$99

3. sweaters
$33

4. cotton blouses
$25

5. leather jackets
$149

6. wash and wear shirts
$22

7. women's hats
$29

8. silk ties
$19

9. belts
$17

1. A: **Will Barbara buy the dress?**
   B: **Yes, she will.**

   A: **Why?**
   B: **Because she really likes it.**

2. A: **Will Joe get rich?**
   B: **No, he won't.**

   A: **Why not?**
   B: **He doesn't have any customers.**

3. Will Ed help Johnnie?

4. Will Brutus eat all the hot dogs?

5. Will Albert catch the bus?

6. Will Maria dance with Peter?

7. Will Mr. Bascomb give his money to the bandit?

8. Will Marty pass the test?

Listen and practice.

WILL AND SHALL: MAKING OFFERS

I'll carry your suitcase.	Shall I answer the phone?
I'll get the sugar for you.	Shall I make some lemonade?

WRITTEN EXERCISE • *Look at the pictures and write in the missing sentences.*

Listen and repeat.

PAIR WORK • *Using these questions, Student A asks for permission to do something. Student B gives or denies permission.*

1. A: **May I borrow your dictionary?**
   B: **Yes, you may.**   OR   **No, I'm sorry.**

Possible affirmative answers:

Yes, you may.
Certainly.
Of course.

Possible negative answers.

No, I'm sorry.
Not now.
Absolutely not!

 *Listen and practice.*

BARBARA: Would you do me a favor, Anne?

ANNE: What is it?

BARBARA: Would you mail these letters for me?

ANNE: No, I can't. I don't have time.

PAIR WORK • *Have similar conversations.*

A: Would you do me a favor, _____?

B: What is it?

A: Would you _____?

B: Yeah, sure. I'll be happy to.
OR   No, I can't. I don't have time.

Include some of these questions in your conversations.

Would you help me with my homework?
_____ return this book to the library?
_____ make me a cup of coffee?
_____ wash the dishes?
_____ clean the windows?
_____ water the plants?
_____ go to the market for me?
_____ carry this suitcase for me?
_____ loan me five dollars?

Possible affirmative answers:

Yeah. (Yes.)
Sure.
OK.
Of course.
No problem.
I'll be happy to.
It's a pleasure.

Possible negative answers:

No.
I'm sorry.
I can't.
Not right now.
I'm busy.
I don't have time.
I'm too tired.

FREE RESPONSE

1. When was the last time you did someone a favor? What was it?
2. When was the last time someone did you a favor? What was it?

CONVERSATION

Listen and practice.

TINO: Would you like to see a movie, Barbara?

BARBARA: No, I went to the movies last night.

TINO: Would you like to go to a dance?

BARBARA: No, not really.

TINO: What would you like to do then?

BARBARA: I'd like to stay home and watch television.

PAIR WORK • *Ask and answer questions using **would like to.** Include some of these suggestions.*

A: Would you like to see a movie, _____?
                go dancing
                play tennis
                go to the park
                visit the museum
                go for a ride
                take a walk
                go swimming

B: No, not really.

A: What would you like to do?

B: I'd like to go home and watch TV.
                get some rest.
                read a book.
                sit by the fire.
                write some letters.
                play the piano.
                listen to music.
                look at some magazines.

1. A: **Would Barney like to meet Ula Hackey?**
   B: **Yes, he would.**
   A: **Why?**
   B: **Because she's a famous movie star.**

2. A: **Would Ed like to have a job?**
   B: **No, he wouldn't.**
   A: **Why not?**
   B: **Because he's lazy.**

3. Would Johnnie like to dance with Gladys?

4. Would Anne like to have an umbrella?

5. Would you like to visit Hawaii?

6. Would you like to eat at Joe's?

7. Would you like to work for Mr. Bascomb?

8. Would you like to be a movie star?

Mr. and Mrs. Bascomb would like to visit Europe this summer. At the moment, they're talking to their travel agent, Mr. Winkle.

"We have three European tours," he says, "Our Grand Tour will be perfect for you. Would you like to see our brochure?"

"Yes, we would," says Mr. Bascomb. "These pictures are lovely. Will the tour include all of Europe, Mr. Winkle?"

"Of course. And you'll have a lot of free time in each country."

"I'd like to know more about the hotels," says Mrs. Bascomb. "Are they first-class?"

"Naturally. You'll stay in the best hotels in Europe. They all have great locations, excellent rooms, and fine cuisine."

"Tell us more about the food," says Mr. Bascomb. "We like to eat well."

"You'll be happy to know all the restaurants on the Grand Tour are famous for their cuisine," says Mr. Winkle. "You can dine when and where you like, even in your room. At no extra charge."

"What about tipping?" asks Mrs. Bascomb. "Is the service included?"

"You don't have to worry about tipping," says Mr. Winkle. "The tour manager pays all the waiters, drivers, and guides."

"Can the tour manager translate for us?" asks Mr. Bascomb. "We don't speak any foreign languages."

"All the tour managers speak several languages. They can help you with anything you need."

"That's wonderful. What do you think, Henrietta? Shall we go?"

"Sure. We can take the tour in June."

"Shall I make your reservations now?" asks Mr. Winkle.

"Yes. Would you like a deposit?"

"Yes, thank you. That will be $500. I know you'll enjoy your trip."

STORY QUESTIONS

1. What would Mr. and Mrs. Bascomb like to do this summer?
2. Who are they talking to right now?
3. How many European tours does Mr. Winkle have?
4. Which tour does he think will be perfect for the Bascombs?
5. Will the Grand Tour include all of Europe?
6. Will they stay in first-class or second-class hotels?
7. What do the best hotels have?
8. Is it necessary to tip the waiters, drivers, and guides?
9. Do the Bascombs need a translator? Why?
10. When would Mrs. Bascomb like to take the tour?
11. Will Mr. Winkle make their reservations today?
12. How much is the deposit?

PAIR WORK • *Barney Field is also going to Europe this summer. He doesn't have much money, so he is traveling on a two-week budget tour. Ask where Barney will be on each day of his trip. Answer by looking at the map.*

> 1. Dublin
> A: **Where will he be on the first day?**
> B: **He'll be in Dublin.**

GROUP WORK • *Plan your dream vacation. Where would you like to go? How long would you like to stay there? What would you like to see and do?*

GROUP WORK • *Discuss the pictures. What do you think will happen in each situation?*

> A: **I think the police officer will catch the robber.**
> B: **I think so, too.**
> C: **I disagree. I think the robber will get away.**
> B: **Why?**
> C: **Because the police officer can't run very fast. He's too slow.**

Listen and practice.

Good evening.

WAITRESS: Good evening. What would you like for dinner?

OTIS: I'll have spaghetti.

WAITRESS: Would you like soup or salad with your dinner?

OTIS: I'd like onion soup.

WAITRESS: Certainly. Anything to drink?

OTIS: Some iced tea, please.

WAITRESS: Yes, sir.

❀ Menu ❀

Soups
- Tomato Soup.. $1.75
- Onion Soup.. $1.75

Salads
- Lettuce & Tomato $1.50
- Mixed Green... $1.80

Dinners
Dinners include your choice of soup or salad

- ROAST BEEF............ $7.95
  served with baked potato & vegetable

- SIRLOIN STEAK........ $6.95
  served with french fries & vegetable

- FRIED CHICKEN........ $5.95
  served with mashed potato & vegetable

- BAKED HAM........... $5.95
  served with sweet potato & vegetable

- SPAGHETTI............ $4.95
  served with garlic bread

Side orders
- Peas.... $1.00
- Carrots.. $.80
- Corn.... $.90
- String beans.. $.90
- French fries.. $1.00
- Onion rings.. $1.00

Beverages
- milk.... $.80
- Coffee... $.60
- Hot tea... $.60
- Iced-tea. $.75
- Orange juice.. $1.00
- Coca-Cola... $.75
- Seven-Up.... $.75

Desserts
- Apple pie... $1.50
- Cheese cake.. $1.75
- Ice cream ... $1.25
- Fruit salad. $1.50

CLASS ACTIVITY • *Where do Ed and Blossom go on their first date? What happens?*

WRITTEN EXERCISE • *Choose a sentence for each picture.*

Are you ready to order?	Could we have the bill, please?	Mmm . . . that looks good.
That was an excellent meal.	What do you recommend?	Thank you.
Good evening.	Good night. Come again.	How is it?

ROLE PLAY • *Work in groups of three. Act out a scene in a restaurant like this one.*

TALKING ABOUT PLACES TO EAT

1. Where is your favorite place to eat?
2. Why do you like it?
3. When is it open?
4. How often do you go there?
5. What kind of food do they serve?
6. What do you usually order?
7. Is it a romantic place?
8. Do they have music? What kind?
9. Is it a good place for conversation?

GROUP WORK • *Talk about your favorite places to eat.*

TALKING ABOUT THE FUTURE

1. Where do you think you'll be a year from now?
2. What are your plans for the future?
3. Do you have any predictions for this year or next year?
4. Who do you think will be the next president or prime minister of your country?
5. What do you think life will be like in the year 2050?

COMPOSITION

1. Write about your favorite place to eat. Why is it special?
2. Write about your dream vacation. Where would you like to go? What would you like to see and do?

Future with WILL Affirmative

He She I You We They	'll (will)	come tomorrow.

Negative

He She I You We They	won't (will not)	come tomorrow.

Interrogative

Will	he she I you we they	come tomorrow?

Short Answers

Yes,	he she I you we they	will.	No,	he she I you we they	won't.

OFFERS

Shall I	make some coffee? play some jazz?

SUGGESTIONS

Shall we	go to the movies? call a taxi?

OFFERS

Would you like	a glass of water? some ice cream?

SUGGESTIONS

Would you like to	go dancing? play tennis?

PERMISSION

May I	use your phone? borrow your pen?

REQUESTS

Would you	open the window? turn off the radio?

Chapter

TOPICS
A bank robbery
At the post office
Health

GRAMMAR
Phrasal verbs
Tag questions
Should

FUNCTIONS
Giving advice
Asking for and giving information

Listen and practice.

Listen and repeat.

Mr. Bascomb <u>postponed</u> his meeting with Peter.

> I don't feel well, Peter. Let's have our meeting next week instead of this week.

He <u>put</u> it <u>off</u> until the following week.

Barbara <u>got</u> a package yesterday.

She <u>picked</u> it <u>up</u> at the post office.

Fred is <u>considering</u> a job at the post office.

He's <u>thinking</u> it <u>over</u> very carefully.

Fred is <u>refusing</u> the job.

He's <u>turning</u> it <u>down</u> because he doesn't like the hours.

PHRASAL VERBS (SEPARABLE)	
We're going to pick up the forms.	We're going to pick them up.
_____ fill out _____.	_____ fill them out.
_____ take back _____.	_____ take them back.
_____ hand in _____.	_____ hand them in.

PRACTICE • *Make sentences using phrasal verbs.*

I like these pants. (try on)	Barney's cab doesn't run very well. (fix up)
I'm going to try them on.	**He's going to fix it up.**

1. Bob thinks Linda is cute. (ask out)
2. My friends must be home now. (call up)
3. Mr. and Mrs. Golo don't want their old clock. (throw out)
4. We borrowed those books from the library. (take back)
5. It's too hot for me to wear this sweater. (take off)
6. My brother's going to be late for work. It's 8:30 and he's still sleeping. (wake up)
7. Rico's girlfriend is waiting for him in front of the bank. (pick up)
8. We have very little money, but we aren't worried. We have a rich uncle. (help out)
9. Don't worry about the money you loaned me. (pay back)

Listen and repeat.

Barney <u>met</u> an old friend yesterday.

He <u>ran into</u> him on Oak Street.

People <u>respect</u> Dr. Pasto.

They <u>look up to</u> him because of his great knowledge.

The famous lawyer, Justin Case, is <u>defending</u> a client.

He's <u>standing up for</u> him in court.

Mr. Bascomb was very sick, but he <u>recovered</u> from his illness.

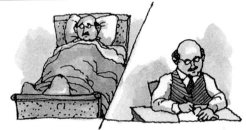

He <u>got over</u> it and went back to work yesterday.

PHRASAL VERBS (INSEPARABLE)	
We looked for Maria at the hospital.	We looked for her at the hospital.
___ waited for _____.	___ waited for _____.
___ called on _____.	___ called on _____.
___ ran into _____.	___ ran into _____.

WRITTEN EXERCISE • *Complete the sentences with the past tense of the phrasal verbs.*

Mr. Bascomb recovered from his illness. He (get over) _*got over*_ it yesterday.

1. Mr. Case defended my neighbor. He (stand up for) _____ him in court.

2. I saw Gloria this morning. I (run into) _____ her at the post office.

3. Mabel returned from the market. She (come back) _____ on the bus.

4. Miss Kelly wrote to us from India. We (hear from) _____ her twice last year.

5. Jimmy finished his homework yesterday. He (get through) _____ all of it.

6. Linda left the house last night. She (go out) _____ with her brother.

7. We visited Peter last week. We (call on) _____ him at his office.

8. Mr. Farley entered the restaurant at 6:30. He (come in) _____ with his wife.

🔊 *Listen and practice.*

SANDY: Hi, Peter. It's a beautiful day, isn't it?

PETER: Yes, it is.

SANDY: You're going to the beach, aren't you?

PETER: Yes, I am.

SANDY: You weren't at the beach yesterday, were you?

PETER: No, I wasn't.

SANDY: You always go by car, don't you?

PETER: Yes, I do.

SANDY: I can't go with you, can I?

PETER: Yes, you can. Get in.

TAG QUESTIONS

You're going to the beach, aren't you?

They're _____, _____ they?

She's _____, isn't she?

He's _____, _____ he?

PRACTICE I • *Add tag questions to these sentences.*

He always goes by car.
He always goes by car, doesn't he?

You stayed home Sunday.
You stayed home Sunday, didn't you?

1. She's a good athlete.
2. She plays a lot of sports.
3. She can run fast.
4. You work hard.
5. You're tired.
6. You need a rest.
7. It was hot yesterday.
8. He went to the beach.
9. He swam in the ocean.

TAG QUESTIONS

You weren't at the beach yesterday, were you?

They _____, _____ they?

She wasn't _____, was she?

He _____, _____ he?

PRACTICE 2 • *Add tag questions to these sentences.*

I can't go with you.
I can't go with you, can I?

She doesn't have a car.
She doesn't have a car, does she?

1. They aren't home now.
2. We can't call them.
3. He isn't a good worker.
4. He doesn't like his job.
5. You didn't go to the store.
6. The store wasn't open.
7. They don't have much money.
8. They aren't going to help us.
9. There isn't enough time.

PAIR WORK I • *Ask and answer tag questions.*

student/study
A: **You're a good student, aren't you?**
B: **Yes, I am.** OR **No, I'm not.**
A: **You study a lot, don't you?**
B: **Yes, I do.** OR **No, I don't.**

1. dancer/dance
2. singer/sing
3. artist/paint
4. student/study
5. cook/cook
6. swimmer/swim
7. tennis player/play tennis

PAIR WORK 2 • *Ask and answer tag questions.*

student/study
A: **You aren't a very good student, are you?**
B: **Yes, I am.** OR **No, I'm not.**
A: **You don't study much, do you?**
B: **Yes, I do.** OR **No, I don't.**

1. dancer/dance
2. singer/sing
3. artist/paint
4. student/study
5. cook/cook
6. swimmer/swim
7. tennis player/play tennis

🔊 *Listen and practice.*

DOCTOR: How are you, Albert?

ALBERT: Not very well, Doctor. I feel tired all the time.

DOCTOR: You should get more sleep.

ALBERT: I get plenty of sleep. But I don't seem to have any energy.

DOCTOR: That's because you're overweight. You shouldn't eat so much.

ALBERT: You mean I should go on a diet?

DOCTOR: That's right. And you should exercise more. Take up a sport.

ALBERT: Well, I was going to play on the basketball team this year. But the coach said I was too slow.

DOCTOR: You should run more to get in shape.

ALBERT: I did a lot of running last year. But it made me very hungry, so I stopped.

DOCTOR: You shouldn't give up, Albert. Just remember, the only way to lose weight is to exercise more and eat less.

ALBERT: Okay, Doctor. I'll do my best.

SHOULD: AFFIRMATIVE
You should get more sleep.
_____ exercise more.
_____ take up a sport.

NEGATIVE
You shouldn't eat so much.
_____ watch so much TV.
_____ stay up late.

WRITTEN EXERCISE • *Choose a sentence for each person. One person has a problem and the other gives advice.*

I have a headache.	You should get some rest.
My back is sore.	You shouldn't play with matches.
I can't sleep.	You should exercise more.
I'm out of shape.	You should take an aspirin.
I burned my finger.	You shouldn't lift heavy objects.
I'm tired.	You shouldn't drink coffee.

PRACTICE • *Make a sentence for each picture, using **should**.*

1. Fred should buy some new shoes.

2. Linda _____.

3. Anne _____.

4. Barney _____.

5. Nick _____.

6. Mrs. Golo _____.

7. Albert _____.

8. Mr. Bascomb _____.

PRACTICE • *Make a sentence for each picture, using **shouldn't**.*

1. Mr. Bascomb shouldn't speak so loudly.

2. Ula Hackey shouldn't spend so much money.

3. Jack _____

4. Sam _____

5. Albert _____

6. Fred _____

7. Johnnie _____

8. Gladys _____

CONVERSATIONS

Listen and practice.

SUZI: Dick and Jane fight a lot, don't they?

NANCY: Yes, they shouldn't fight so much.

SUZI: Why don't you talk with them? Maybe they'll listen to you.

NANCY: *You* talk with them. They're *your* friends.

OTIS: Peter drives very fast, doesn't he?

GLORIA: Yes, he shouldn't drive so fast.

OTIS: Why don't you talk with him? Maybe he'll listen to you.

GLORIA: *You* talk with him. He's *your* friend.

PAIR WORK • *Have similar conversations.*

1. Albert eats a lot, doesn't he?

2. Ms. Fern works very hard, doesn't she?

3. Joe and Eddie smoke a lot, don't they?

4. Mr. Bascomb speaks loudly, doesn't he?

5. Mr. and Mrs. Farley drink a lot of coffee, don't they?

6. Betty spends a lot of money, doesn't she?

It's 12:30. There's a hold-up at the City Bank. One of the bandits is pointing a gun at Miss Jones. She's very frightened.

"Give me all the large bills," he says.

"Do you want them in a bag?"

"No. Just hand them to me. And don't try to call for help."

"I'm not dumb enough to do anything like that," says Miss Jones. "Besides, we always try to please our customers. Right, Mr. Bascomb?"

Another bandit is giving orders to Mr. Bascomb. "Take me to the safe," he says. "And then open it for me."

"All right," says Mr. Bascomb. "But there's hardly anything in it." He's very worried. He hopes the police will come soon.

A third bandit is standing at the entrance to the bank. He's calling to his friends. "Let's go. We don't have much time. The police will be here in a few minutes."

STORY QUESTIONS

1. What time is it?
2. What's happening at the City Bank?
3. Why is Anne frightened?
4. What does the bandit say to her?
5. Why doesn't she call for help?
6. What does the second bandit say to Mr. Bascomb?
7. Is there much money in the safe?
8. What does Mr. Bascomb hope will happen?
9. Where is the third bandit?
10. Why is he calling to his friends?

GROUP WORK • *Talk about the picture. Then write down your observations. Share them with your class.*

FREE RESPONSE

1. Who is the detective talking to?
2. Where are they?
3. How does Buster feel?
4. What do you think Buster did?
5. Do you think he acted alone?
6. What kind of car do you think Buster drives?
7. What kind of food do you think he likes to eat?
8. What kind of music do you think he enjoys?
9. What do you think Buster likes to do in his free time?
10. Do you think Buster will enjoy himself in the future?

ROLE PLAY • *What do you think the detective is saying to Buster? Make up a dialogue between Buster and the detective. Act out the scene before the class.*

Listen and practice.

CLYDE: May I help you?

ANNE: I'd like to send this package to *Florida*.

CLYDE: How do you want to send it?

ANNE: *First class.*

CLYDE: Let's see. It weighs *three pounds eleven ounces*. That'll be *four dollars and sixty-five cents*.

ANNE: Oh, that's expensive.

CLYDE: You can send it *fourth class* for *one dollar and sixty-six cents*.

ANNE: How long does it take?

CLYDE: First class takes two or three days. Fourth class takes about a week.

ANNE: Send it fourth class, please.

PAIR WORK • *Have similar conversations. Decide if you want to send your package first class or fourth class.*

1. 4 lbs. 7 ounces
   first class/$5.35
   fourth class/$1.72

2. 5 lbs. 8 ounces
   first class/$5.65
   fourth class/$1.89

3. 3 lbs. 12 ounces
   first class/$4.55
   fourth class/$1.66

4. 6 lbs. 9 ounces
   first class/$6.00
   fourth class/$2.01

5. 2 lbs. 10 ounces
   first class/$4.00
   fourth class/$1.54

6. 5 lbs. 2 ounces
   first class/$5.43
   fourth class/$1.78

PAIR WORK • *Ask and answer questions.*

> A: **You have a bicycle, don't you?**
> B: **Yes, I do.**   OR   **No, I don't.**

1. You're very busy, aren't you?
2. You don't have much free time, do you?
3. You aren't thinking about the weekend, are you?
4. You were at home last night, weren't you?
5. You didn't watch TV, did you?
6. You like classical music, don't you?
7. You can't play the guitar, can you?
8. You went to a movie yesterday, didn't you?
9. You weren't at the library, were you?

WRITTEN EXERCISE • *Complete each sentence with the most appropriate phrasal verb in the box. Use each phrasal verb only once.*

come back	pick up	turn down
fix up	put off	turn on
hear from	ran into	wake up
help out	throw out	write down

> It's hot in here. Let's _*turn on*_ the air conditioner.
>
> I want to sleep. Please don't _*wake*_ me _*up*_.

1. We don't want that old coffee pot. We're going to _____ it _____.
2. I need your address. Can you _____ it _____ for me?
3. You should take your vacation now. Don't _____ it _____.
4. I hope you'll send me a post card. I'd like to _____ you.
5. Rufus was very surprised when he _____ Gloria at the market yesterday.
6. He asked her for a date, but she _____ him _____.
7. My brother's leaving tomorrow and will _____ on Friday.
8. I'm going to _____ him _____ at the airport when he returns.
9. My car is in bad condition. I have to _____ it _____.
10. I don't have enough money to pay for repairs. Can you _____ me _____?

FREE RESPONSE

1. What do you usually have for breakfast? Do you ever have breakfast in bed?
2. What do people usually eat for breakfast in your country?
3. Is it hard for you to get to work or school on time? How long does it take?
4. What are your plans for Saturday? Are you going to stay home or go out?
5. Do you like to dress up? How do you dress when you go to a party?
6. What do you wear when you want to be comfortable?
7. Are you saving your money to buy something? What is it?
8. Do you need to buy anything for your home?
9. Do you have a lot of housework? What kind of chores do you do at home?

🔊 *Listen and practice*

DR. CHANG: What's the matter?

RODNEY: I have a cold.

DR. CHANG: You should take vitamin C.

RODNEY: I've already tried that. It didn't help.

DR. CHANG: What's the matter?

MR. BASCOMB: I have insomnia.

DR. CHANG: Do you drink coffee?

MR. BASCOMB: Yes, it's my favorite drink.

DR. CHANG: Well, you shouldn't drink coffee, especially at night.

MR. BASCOMB: Okay. I'll take your advice.

PAIR WORK • *You're at the doctor's office. Student A has a problem. Student B gives advice.*

TALKING ABOUT HEALTH

1. Do you take good care of yourself?
2. What kind of food is necessary for good health?
3. Do you eat a lot of fruit and vegetables? What about meat? fish? milk?
4. Do you take vitamins? What is vitamin C good for?
5. Do you exercise regularly? Do you swim, jog, or play a sport?
6. How do you relax?
7. How much sleep do you get? Is that enough?
8. What causes a headache? a stomachache? a sunburn?
9. Do you have a family doctor? Does your doctor give you good advice?
10. Did you ever stay in a hospital? If so, what happened to you?

ROLE PLAY • *Student A is a doctor. Student B is a patient.*
Situation: The patient feels tired. The doctor asks if the patient gets enough sleep, eats the right kind of food, gets enough exercise, and so on.

COMPOSITION • *What should a person do to stay healthy?*

PHRASAL VERBS (INSEPARABLE)

We're	looking waiting	for	Maria. our friends.		We're	looking waiting	for	her. them.

PHRASAL VERBS (SEPARABLE)

He's	picking up putting away	the newspaper. the magazines.		He's	picking putting	the newspaper the magazines	up. away.

He's	picking it up. putting them away.

TAG QUESTIONS Affirmative

It's a beautiful day,	isn't it?
They're going to the beach,	aren't they?
You have an umbrella,	don't you?
She was at the movies,	wasn't she?
He can play the piano,	can't he?
He likes music,	doesn't he?

Negative

There aren't any matches,	are there?
He isn't working today,	is he?
They don't like football,	do they?
You weren't at the party,	were you?
She can't drive a truck,	can she?
He doesn't have a telephone,	does he?

SHOULD Affirmative

I He You	should	get up earlier. exercise more. study harder.

Negative

She We They	shouldn't (should not)	drive so fast. spend so much money. forget so easily.

Interrogative

Should	I call the hospital? we leave at five o'clock? he take his car?

Short Answers

Yes,	you we he	should.		No,	you we he	shouldn't.

Chapter

TOPICS
Accidents
Emergencies
Meeting people

GRAMMAR
Ago/how long ago?
Must (obligation)
Past continuous

FUNCTIONS
Describing a situation in the past
Expressing obligation
Describing an accident
Requesting assistance
Starting a conversation

1

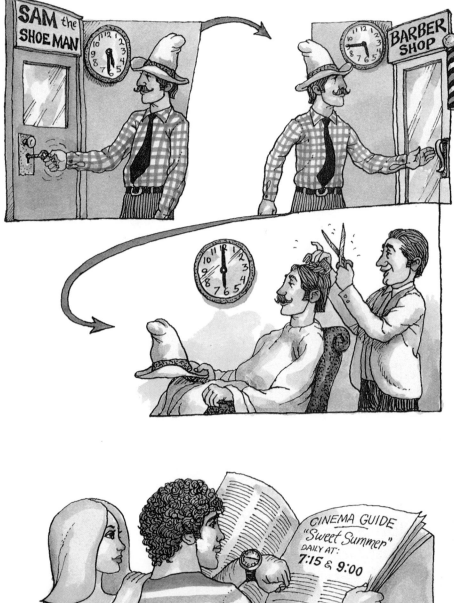

2

1. *Talk about the pictures.*
2. *Listen to the stories.*
3. *Answer the story questions.*

READING

1 Mr. Brown left his shop at 5:30. Then he went to the barber shop. He arrived there at 5:45. That was 15 minutes ago. It's 6 o'clock now.

1. What time did Sam leave his shop?
2. What time did he arrive at the barber shop?
3. What time is it now?
4. How long ago did Sam leave his shop?
5. How long ago did he arrive at the barber shop?

2 It's 9:15. Tino and Barbara would like to see a film called *Sweet Summer.* They're looking at the cinema guide. The first show began at 7:15. The second show began at 9 o'clock.

1. What time is it?
2. What would Tino and Barbara like to see?
3. How long ago did the first show begin?
4. How long ago did the second show begin?
5. Is it too late to see the entire film?

AGO
Sam left his shop fifteen minutes ago.
_____ half an hour ago.
_____ an hour ago.
_____ a long time ago.

WRITTEN EXERCISE • *Complete the sentences with a verb in the past tense. Add a preposition when necessary.*

Sam *went to* the barber shop a little while ago.
Linda *finished* her homework half an hour ago.

1. Barney _____ his car a couple of weeks ago.
2. We _____ the museum a few weeks ago.
3. Mr. Bascomb _____ breakfast an hour ago.
4. He _____ the newspaper a little while ago.
5. He _____ the bank a few minutes ago.
6. Mrs. Golo _____ a bath an hour ago.
7. She _____ the dog fifteen minutes ago.
8. She _____ the dishes a long time ago.
9. Maria _____ a letter a few days ago.
10. She _____ the rent a week ago.
11. I _____ my brother a little while ago.
12. He _____ a haircut a few days ago.

Listen and practice.

MR. BASCOMB: Have you got a book called *Modern Banking?*

JOHNNIE WILSON: I sold the last copy two months ago.

MR. BASCOMB: Did you order more copies of the book?

JOHNNIE WILSON: Yes, I did.

MR. BASCOMB: How long ago did you order them?

JOHNNIE WILSON: About a week ago.

MRS. BROWN: Was Sam here today?

BARBER: Yes, he was. He came for a haircut.

MRS. BROWN: I must find him. Do you know where he went?

BARBER: Yes. I think he went to Nick's Garage. It's not far from here.

MRS. BROWN: How long ago did he leave?

BARBER: He left fifteen minutes ago. He must be there now.

Note: I must find him. = I have to find him.
He must be there. = He's probably there.

PAIR WORK • *It's twelve o'clock. Ask and answer questions about the pictures.*

1. A: **How long ago did Barney get up?**
   B: **He got up three and a half hours ago.**

2. How long ago did he eat breakfast?

3. How long ago did Anne clean the kitchen?

4. How long ago did she read the newspaper?

5. How long ago did Otis call Gloria?

6. How long ago did he pick her up?

7. How long ago did they arrive at Mom's?

8. How long ago did they leave Mom's?

1

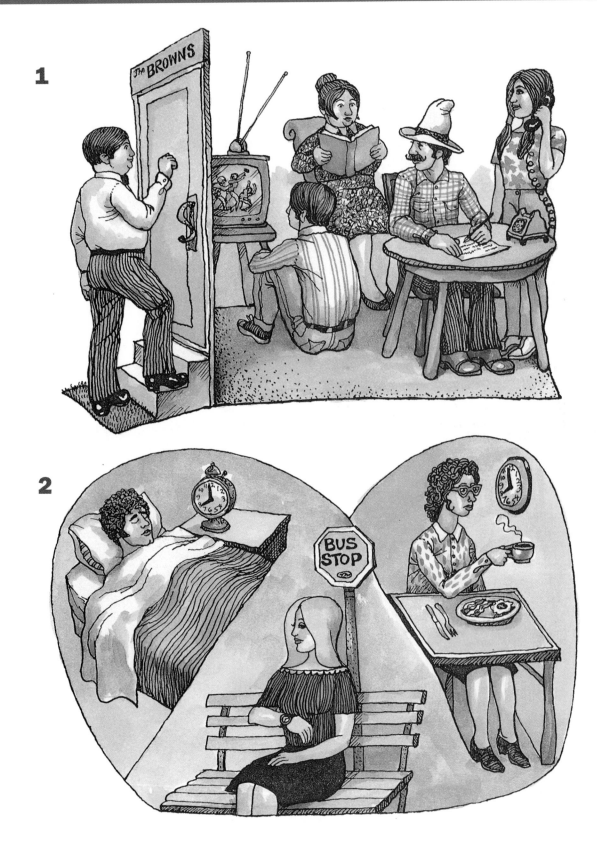

2

1. *Talk about the pictures.*
2. *Listen to the stories.*
3. *Answer the story questions.*

READING

1 Last night Albert visited the Brown family. When he arrived, Mr. Brown was writing letters and his wife was reading a book. Jimmy was watching television and Linda was talking on the phone.

1. Who did Albert visit last night?
2. What was Mr. Brown doing when he arrived?
3. What was Mrs. Brown doing?
4. What was Jimmy doing?
5. What was Linda doing?

2 At eight o'clock this morning Tino was sleeping. At the same time, Barbara was waiting for the bus and Anne was having breakfast.

1. What was Tino doing at eight o'clock this morning?
2. What was Barbara doing while Tino was sleeping?
3. What was Anne doing while Barbara was waiting for the bus?
4. Was Tino sleeping while Barbara was waiting for the bus?

PAST CONTINUOUS	
He was sleeping at eight o'clock.	They were working this morning.
_____ getting up _____.	_____ studying _____.
_____ taking a shower _____.	_____ reading _____.
_____ eating breakfast _____.	_____ writing _____.

PRACTICE • *Answer the questions.*

What was Anne doing at eight o'clock? (having breakfast)
She was having breakfast.

What were Nick and Barney doing this morning? (working)
They were working.

1. What was Barbara doing at eight o'clock? (waiting for the bus)
2. What was she doing at ten o'clock? (working at the bank)
3. What was she doing at one o'clock? (having lunch with Tino)
4. What were Jimmy and his friends doing this morning? (studying at the library)
5. What were they doing this afternoon? (playing basketball)
6. What was Jack doing at the park yesterday? (feeding the birds)
7. What was Peter doing at the hospital yesterday? (visiting Maria)
8. What were the Browns doing last weekend? (cleaning the house)
9. What were they doing last night? (watching television)

Listen and practice.

PAIR WORK • *Have similar conversations.*

1. Nancy

2. Fred and Barney

3. Otis

4. Barbara and Tino

5. Suzi Suzuki

6. David and Janet

7. Nick

8. Jimmy and Linda

9. Anne

CONVERSATION

Listen and practice.

JACK: What did you do last night, Sam?

SAM: I wrote some letters. And you?

JACK: While you were writing letters, I was working at the snack bar.

SAM: Oh, really?

PAIR WORK • *Have similar conversations.*

A: What did you do last night (this morning), _____?

B: I _____. And you?

A: While you were _____, I was _____.

B: Oh, really?

Include some of these activities.

listen to the radio	read a magazine
play cards	do my homework
watch television	have breakfast or dinner
work in the garden	take a walk in the park
talk on the phone	clean the house or apartment
play tennis	study at the library
work at the office	write some letters
watch the football game	dance at the Disco Club

A few months ago Peter Smith had an accident. He was driving to work when a dog ran in front of his car. He turned sharply and missed the dog, but his car hit a tree. A police officer was standing on the corner when the accident happened. He called an ambulance immediately. The attendants came and took Peter to the hospital. While they were driving to the hospital, Peter was talking about the accident. "The dog caused the accident," said Peter. "It wasn't my fault."

Peter Smith stayed in the hospital for a month. But he wasn't sad. While he was in the hospital, Peter was planning his next trip to Europe. "I'm going to visit France, and then go to Germany," he said. "Germany is beautiful in the fall."

The nurse smiled. "That's wonderful," she said. "You're lucky you can travel to so many interesting places."

STORY QUESTIONS

1. When did Peter have the accident?
2. Where was he going when the dog ran in front of his car?
3. Did Peter hit the dog?
4. Did he hit anything?
5. Who was standing on the corner when the accident happened?
6. What did he do?
7. Where did the attendants take Peter?
8. What was Peter talking about while they were driving to the hospital?
9. Was the accident Peter's fault?
10. How long did Peter stay in the hospital?
11. What was he thinking about while he was in the hospital?
12. What countries does Peter plan to visit?
13. Do you think Peter is lucky or unlucky?

WRITTEN EXERCISE • *Write a sentence for each road sign. Use each sentence only once.*

You must stop.   You must keep to the right.   You must turn right.
You must not park.   You must not enter.   You must not make a U turn.
You must not turn left.   You must turn left.

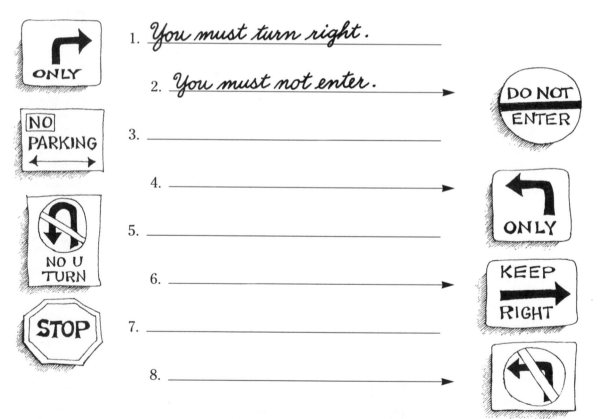

1. *You must turn right.*

2. *You must not enter.*

3. _____

4. _____

5. _____

6. _____

7. _____

8. _____

Must in the affirmative has almost the same meaning as **have to:**
   You must go = You have to go.
Must in the negative has the same meaning as a negative command:
   You must not go = Don't go.

• *Ask and answer questions about the pictures.*

1. A: **What was the police officer doing when the accident happened?**
   B: **He was standing on the corner.**

2. A: **What were the Browns doing when it started to rain?**
   B: **They were having a picnic.**

3. What were the boys doing when their mother called them?

4. What was Barbara doing when Tino arrived?

5. What was Johnnie doing when the telephone rang?

6. What were the girls doing when Marty came into the room?

7. What were the girls doing when Marty left?

8. What was Gloria doing when Otis called the waiter?

WRITTEN EXERCISE • *Write questions using* **who, what,** *or* **where.**

Barbara was waiting for the bus. *What was she waiting for?*

She was talking to Anne. *Who was she talking to?*

They were going to the museum. *Where were they going?*

1. Otis and Gloria were having lunch at Mom's Cafe. _____

2. Gloria was wearing a green dress. _____

3. They were talking about Dr. Pasto. _____

4. Sam was writing a letter to his brother. _____

5. Mabel was cleaning the kitchen. _____

6. Albert and Linda were studying at the library. _____

7. They were listening to the radio. _____

8. Nancy was talking to Barney on the phone. _____

9. The boys were playing football in the park. _____

FREE RESPONSE

1. What were you wearing yesterday?
2. Who were you talking to on the phone last night?
3. Why were you smiling this morning?

PAIR WORK 1 • *Ask and answer questions using the past continuous.*

this morning at ten o'clock
A: **What were you doing this morning at ten o'clock?**
B: **I was walking to the library.** OR **I was reading a book.**

1. this morning at eight o'clock
2. last night at seven o'clock
3. last night at ten-thirty
4. at this time yesterday
5. at noon yesterday
6. at this time last year

PAIR WORK 2 • *Ask and answer questions.*

ride a bicycle
A: **When was the last time you rode a bicycle?**
B: **The last time was about ten years ago.**
   OR **I rode a bicycle two weeks ago.**

1. write a letter
2. read a good book
3. go to a movie
4. eat in a restaurant
5. take a vacation
6. play basketball
7. go to a party
8. lose something
9. have an accident

Listen and practice.

OPERATOR:	Emergency. Can I help you?
MRS. GRANT:	Yes! *My husband is choking!*
OPERATOR:	What's your address?
MRS. GRANT:	*Eighteen-eleven Rock Street.*
OPERATOR:	Your name, please.
MRS. GRANT:	*Betty Grant.*
OPERATOR:	Help is on the way.

PAIR WORK • *Have similar conversations. Call for help and say what happened. Then give the address where it happened and your name.*

1. There's a prowler in my backyard!
   579 Maple Street

2. My house is on fire!
   3246 Sunset Avenue

3. Someone stole my car!
   1430 Franklin Avenue

4. My father is unconscious!
   2067 Lime Street

5. There's smoke coming from my neighbor's house!
   1154 Dixon Avenue

6. Someone just robbed my sister!
   825 Main Street

• *These pictures show how some of the characters in this book met for the first time. Choose a sentence for each picture.*

Who's winning?	How are the apples?	What are you reading?
That's a nice painting.	Would you like to dance?	Beautiful day, isn't it?

1. Sandy — Peter

2. Jenny — Marty

3. Otis — Gloria

4. Candy — Rico

5. George — Betty

6. Linda — Bob

PAIR WORK 1 • *Ask and answer questions about the people in the pictures using the past continuous.*

> 1. Sandy — Peter
> A: **What was Sandy doing when she met Peter?**
> B: **She was buying apples at the market.**

PAIR WORK 2 • *Choose one of the couples in the pictures and make up a conversation. Use the model below.*

PETER: How are the apples?
SANDY: _____ .

PETER: Do you come here often?
SANDY: Yes, this is my favorite store. I like it because _____ .

PETER: That's why I come here. Say, what's your name?
SANDY: Sandy.

Continue the conversation. Ask more questions.

FREE RESPONSE

1. Are you getting together with anyone tonight or tomorrow? What do you plan to do?
2. Do you like to dance? Do you know a good place for dancing?
3. Do you like to sing? What's your favorite song?
4. When was the last time you went to a party? What did you do at the party?
5. Do you ever borrow things from your friends? When was the last time you borrowed something?
6. What did you do yesterday morning? yesterday afternoon?
7. When was the last time you saw a good movie? What was it about?
8. How often do you write letters. Who do you write to? Can you write a letter in English?
9. How often do you speak English outside of class? How many of your friends speak English?

ONE STEP FURTHER

This picture shows Barbara and Tino two years ago, when they first met.

FREE RESPONSE

1. How did Barbara and Tino meet?
2. Who do you think spoke first?
3. What do you think they said to each other?

ROLE PLAY

Student A plays Barbara. Student B plays Tino.
Situation: They're in a cafe. They meet for the first time. Make up a short conversation.

TALKING ABOUT MEETING PEOPLE

1. Is it easy or difficult to meet people where you live?
2. Where and how do people usually meet?
3. Do you remember when you met a special person in your life? Where were you? What were you doing? How did you meet?

COMPOSITION • *Write about a time you met a special person in your life. Give the details.*

Interrogative	
How long ago	did the movie start?
	did they leave?

Affirmative	
It started	a few minutes ago.
They left	a little while ago.
	half an hour ago.

HAVE TO		
He She	has to	get up early.
I You We They	have to	go to the market. buy some food.

MUST		
He She I You We They	must	get up early. go to the market. buy some food.

PAST CONTINUOUS: Affirmative			
He She I	was	sleeping working	when the telephone rang.
You We They	were	reading studying	while it was raining.

Negative			
He She I	wasn't (was not)	sleeping working	when the telephone rang.
You We They	weren't (were not)	reading studying	while it was raining.

Interrogative		
Was	he she I	sleeping? working?
Were	you we they	reading? studying?

Short Answers					
Yes,	he she I	was.	No,	he she I	wasn't.
	you we they	were.		you we they	weren't.

Review Chapter

8

TOPICS
Directions
Nutrition
Shopping
Recipes
Your hometown

GRAMMAR
Review

FUNCTIONS
Making logical conclusions
Asking the way and giving directions
Declining invitations and making excuses
Showing concern
Taking telephone messages
Asking a favor and responding
Giving instructions

Yesterday Sam Brown was talking to a visitor when Albert came into the room.

"Mr. Brown," he said, "I have to talk with you."

"Of course, Albert. Would you like some hot chocolate and cake?"

"Yes, thank you, Mr. Brown." Albert was breathing hard. "I heard that you're going to sell your house and move to a farm in the country. Is it true?"

"Yes, it is, Albert. I was just talking to Mr. Fix about it. He's the real estate agent. We were looking at some photos of farmland and . . ."

"But Mr. Brown, why are you selling your house and moving away?" Albert looked very unhappy.

"Well, Albert, Wickam City is getting too big for me. There are too many people in this town, and there isn't enough room to breathe. Besides, Mabel and I always wanted to live on a farm."

Just then Mabel came into the room. She was carrying a large tray of lemonade, hot chocolate, cookies, homemade candy, and cake.

"Hello, Albert," she said. "It's nice to see you. We have lemonade and hot chocolate. Which would you prefer?"

"I'll have both, thank you," said Albert. He was very hungry, as usual.

"And you, Mr. Fix?" she said. Mabel was a good hostess and always thought of her guests.

"Neither one for me," he said. "I don't want any."

Mr. Fix looked at Albert. Albert was drinking lemonade while balancing a cup of hot chocolate on his right knee and a plate full of cake and cookies on his left knee.

"You must be very thirsty," he said.

"I am," said Albert. He finished all of the lemonade and then drank the hot chocolate. After that he picked up a piece of cake.

"I made a lot of cake," said Mabel, "so eat all you want."

"I will," said Albert.

"Okay," said Mr. Fix. "But I never eat much before dinner."

"I'm afraid the cookies aren't very good this time," said Mabel. "I left them in the oven too long and they're a little dry."

"That's okay, I'll eat them anyway," said Albert, taking another handful.

"Oh, Mabel," laughed Sam, "you're just looking for compliments. Everything tastes pretty good to me."

"I guess I will have a little cake," said Mr. Fix. "And now Mr. Brown, let's talk business. I have two pieces of property here. One has a lot of land, with fruit trees and animals on it. But there aren't any towns nearby. The only town in the area is Colterville, and it's about fifty miles away. The other piece of property is quite small and doesn't have any fruit trees or animals, but it's close to town. Which one would you like?"

"Well," said Sam, "Mabel and I were talking it over and we decided to take the first piece of property, the one that's a long way from town, with the animals and fruit trees."

"That's right, Mr. Fix," said Mabel. "It looks so peaceful there."

"When will the farm be available?" asked Sam.

"In about three weeks."

Just then Albert coughed. Everyone turned and looked at him.

"Why Albert," cried Mabel. "You ate all the cake and cookies."

"That's incredible," said Mr. Fix. "I didn't think it was possible."

"You aren't making a very good impression," said Sam. He was disappointed in Albert.

"I'm sorry," said Albert. "But Mr. and Mrs. Brown, you can't move to the country."

"Why not, Albert?" asked Mabel.

"I think I know," said Sam, smiling. "Don't worry, Albert. Linda is still going to the University. She'll stay here and live with the Golos. You can see her whenever you want."

"Well, that's nice," said Albert. "There's something else, though."

"What's that, Albert?" asked Mabel.

"If you move to the country, I can't eat here anymore," replied Albert, reaching for another piece of candy. "I'm sure going to miss your cooking, Mrs. Brown."

STORY QUESTIONS

1. Who was Sam talking to when Albert came into the room?
2. What were they looking at?
3. Why does Sam want to leave Wickam City and move to a farm?
4. Who came into the room while Sam was talking to Albert?
5. What was she carrying on her tray?
6. Did Albert want lemonade or hot chocolate?
7. What did Mr. Fix want?
8. How many pieces of property does Mr. Fix have?
9. What's the first piece of property like?
10. What's the second one like?
11. Which piece of property did Sam and Mabel decide to take?
12. Why is Albert unhappy that the Browns are leaving Wickam City?
13. Where is Linda going to live?
14. Would you like to live on a farm? Why or why not?

PRACTICE • *Make sentences using **must be** + adjective.*

Albert is eating a lot.	Anyone can learn to ride a bicycle.
He must be hungry.	**It must be easy.**

1. Everyone wants to read that book.
2. It takes a long time to learn Russian.
3. Dr. Pasto can discuss anything.
4. People think Barbara looks like a movie star.
5. Fred always makes the same mistake.
6. Mrs. Hamby has to wear very large clothes.
7. Tino has a good job and a beautiful girlfriend.
8. The Martinoli Restaurant always has a lot of customers.
9. Mr. Bascomb doesn't have time for anything.

WRITTEN EXERCISE • *Complete the sentences using the past continuous and the past simple.*

Sam (talk) *was talking* to a visitor when Albert (arrive) *arrived* .

We (walk) *were walking* home when we (hear) *heard* a loud noise.

1. The passengers (sleep) _____ when the plane (land) _____ .

2. Peter (drive) _____ to work when he (have) _____ an accident.

3. Anne (work) _____ at the bank when the telegram (arrive) _____ .

4. Otis and Gloria (take) _____ their seats when the movie (start) _____ .

5. Daisy (clean) _____ the kitchen when Simon (appear) _____ at the door.

6. Sam (make) _____ breakfast when Mabel (get up) _____ this morning.

7. They (have) _____ a conversation when Jimmy (enter) _____ the room.

8. We (play) _____ cards when our friends (call) _____ .

9. Nancy (take) _____ a shower when the phone (ring) _____ .

10. Mr. Hamby (travel) _____ in Mexico when he (get) _____ sick.

11. Gloria (wash) _____ the dishes when she (drop) _____ the plate.

12. I (do) _____ my homework when you (turn on) _____ the radio.

FREE RESPONSE • *What do you think is going to happen in these situations? Make sentences using* **going to.**

Ann is walking to the post office.
She's going to mail a letter.
OR **She's going to buy some stamps.**

1. Linda is tired.
2. Albert is hungry.
3. Nancy has a headache.
4. Barney's clothes are dirty.
5. Mabel is going to the market.
6. Fred needs some money.
7. Maria is looking for the shampoo.
8. Tino is picking up the phone.
9. The girls are looking at the cinema guide.
10. The sky is full of black clouds.

PAIR WORK • *Ask and answer questions using the past tense.*

take my magazine
A: **Did you take my magazine?**
B: **No, I didn't. Someone else took your magazine.**

1. eat my sandwich
2. drink my soda
3. take my money
4. clean the kitchen
5. open the window
6. drop the vase
7. write that letter
8. borrow my dictionary
9. use my shampoo

Wickam City is an average-sized town in California. It's not far from the mountains, and it takes only a few minutes to drive to the ocean. The weather is excellent, with a lot of sunshine and only a few days of rain during the winter months. It hardly ever snows in the city, but there is plenty of snow in the mountains from December to April.

The residents of Wickam City are lucky in many respects. They have clean air, and there isn't much traffic or noise. Public transportation is very good. A lot of people take the bus to work, and some even ride their bicycles. Wickam City has many pleasant, uncrowded streets. And there is almost no pollution. That's because there isn't much industry, just an old ice cream factory on Clark Street.

Although Wickam City doesn't have much green space, there is a beautiful park on the east side called City Park. It's a popular place for picnics and family outings. People in Wickam City really enjoy nature and try to take advantage of the natural beauty that surrounds them. At certain times of the year, during the late fall and spring months, it's possible to ski in the mountains and swim in the ocean, all in the same day.

The mountains and beaches are excellent tourist attractions. However, there isn't much tourism in Wickam City because the town has only a few first-class hotels. Most visitors stay at the Wickam Hotel on Third Avenue.

Wickam City has a good police department and there is very little crime. It's true there was a holdup at the City Bank a few weeks ago, but the police found the robbers and returned all the money. Mr. Bascomb was very happy about that.

Wickam City has a lot of entertainment, and everyone likes to go out and have a good time. There are a lot of theaters and restaurants in the downtown area, and they are usually filled with people on the weekends. Unfortunately, there aren't many nightclubs or discotheques in town. The only good place for dancing is the Disco Club on Rock Street.

People in Wickam City love sports and are very proud of their football team, the Wickam Warriors. There is also a lot of interest in music and the arts. This month they are having an important exhibition at the Art Museum, featuring paintings by famous European artists, including Picasso. In the summer, people enjoy concerts at the open-air theater in City Park. The Symphony Orchestra gives a lot of free performances there.

Ordinarily residents of Wickam City are not very interested in politics, but this is an election year. The current mayor, Frank Connors, is retiring after eight years in office. The people will vote for a new mayor this fall. So far, the only candidate for the job is John Bascomb, president of City Bank.

STORY QUESTIONS

1. What state is Wickam City in?
2. Is Wickam City a good place to live? Why or why not?
3. How is the weather in Wickam City?
4. What is public transportation like?
5. How much traffic and noise is there?
6. Why isn't there much pollution in Wickam City?
7. Why isn't there much tourism?
8. Is crime a big problem in Wickam City?
9. What happened to the robbers who held up City Bank?
10. What kind of entertainment does Wickam City have?
11. Is there much interest in music and the arts?
12. What about politics?
13. Why are people interested in politics this year?

PAIR WORK 1 • *Ask and answer questions about your hometowns.*

> parks
> A: **Are there many parks in your hometown?**
> B: **Yes, there are a lot of parks in my hometown.**
> **(No, there aren't many, only a few, very few.)**
> **(No, there aren't any, there are none.)**
>
> tourism
> A: **Is there much tourism in your hometown?**
> B: **Yes, there's a lot of tourism in my hometown.**
> **(No, there isn't much, only a little, very little.)**
> **(No, there isn't any, there's none.)**

1. banks	5. hotels	9. pollution
2. factories	6. restaurants	10. libraries
3. industry	7. traffic	11. theaters
4. crime	8. noise	12. entertainment

PAIR WORK 2 • *Look at the picture on page 133. Ask for and give directions.*

> barber shop → Olson's Department Store
> A: **Excuse me. How can I get to Olson's Department Store from here?**
> B: **Go to Main Street, turn right, go (up) one block to Star Avenue, and you'll see it across the street.**
>
> Rex Theater → drug store
> A: **Excuse me. How can I get to the drug store from here?**
> B: **Go (down) two blocks to Lime Street, turn left, and you'll see it next to the church.**

1. drug store → post office	7. Grand Hotel → barber shop
2. bookstore → City Park	8. supermarket → post office
3. flower shop → Rex Theater	9. Rex Theater → flower shop
4. post office → State Bank	10. gas station → Mom's Cafe
5. parking lot → gas station	11. barber shop → Grand Hotel
6. Mom's Cafe → bookstore	12. church → Olson's Department Store

Listen and practice.

NANCY: Hi, Barney. We're having a picnic this Saturday. Would you like to come?

BARNEY: Oh, I'd like to, but I can't. I have to take my sister to the airport.

NANCY: That's too bad. It's going to be a great picnic.

BARNEY: Well, maybe next time. Thanks anyway.

Hi, Barney.

PAIR WORK • *Have similar conversations. Student A invites Student B to a social event, such as a picnic or a party. Student B declines the invitation and gives an excuse for not going. Here are some possible excuses:*

I have to study for an exam.
_____ do some shopping.
_____ clean the house (or apartment).
_____ help my father (or mother).
_____ do my homework.

_____ go to a meeting.
_____ work at the office.
_____ do some laundry.
_____ get ready for a trip.
_____ go out of town.

WRITTEN EXERCISE • *Complete the sentences using these adverbs:* **safely, slowly, hard, quickly, beautifully, easily, loudly, peacefully, immediately, dangerously, softly.** *Use each adverb only once.*

Nancy walks *quickly*. She's always in a hurry.

1. Mr. and Mrs. Holt spoke _____ because their daughter was sleeping.

2. When the doctor found out the baby was sick, he came _____.

3. It takes Anne a long time to type a letter. She types very _____.

4. We complained because some people were talking _____ in the theater.

5. Natalya and Boris dance _____ together because they practice all the time.

6. I won't go anywhere with Jack because he drives _____.

7. Mr. Poole was worried about the children, but they returned home _____.

8. My sister has a quiet life. She lives _____ in a small town in the country.

9. If you want to be successful, you have to work _____.

10. This exercise isn't difficult. You can do it _____.

Listen and practice.

ANNE: You look worried. Is something wrong?

BARBARA: I'm concerned about Mr. Bascomb. He takes too many pills.

ANNE: I know. It's terrible.

PAIR WORK • *Have similar conversations.*

A: You look worried. Is something wrong?

B: I'm concerned about _____.

He/she _____ too much/too many _____.

A: I know. It's terrible.

OR That's too bad. I'm sorry to hear that.

OR That's nothing. Forget it.

OR Don't worry. He'll/She'll be all right.

1. Mrs. Farley
   eat/chocolates

2. Johnnie
   drink/coffee

3. Gladys
   smoke/cigarettes

4. George
   watch/TV

5. Marty
   read/comic books

6. Betty
   spend/money

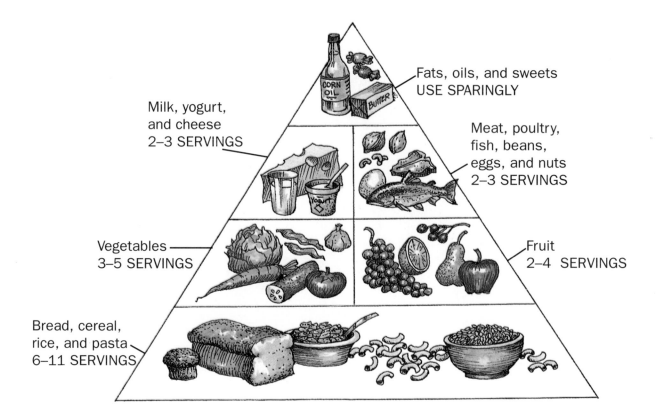

The *food pyramid* classifies foods into six basic groups. It also tells you how many daily servings from each group you need to stay healthy. At the bottom of the food pyramid, you can find the bread, cereal, rice, and pasta group. This group supplies *energy* and important *vitamins* and *minerals* for the body. The next two groups are the fruit and vegetable groups. They also supply important vitamins and minerals.

Next is the dairy group. It includes milk, yogurt, and cheese. To the right of the dairy group you will find the meat, poultry, fish, beans, eggs, and nuts group. Both of these groups are important sources of *protein*, which the body needs for growth.

The last group at the top of the pyramid is the fats, oils, and sweets group. You shouldn't eat too many of these foods because they aren't good for the body. In order to be healthy, you should choose foods from the lower food groups. By eating the right amount of these foods every day, you will get all the *nutrients* you need.

FREE RESPONSE

1. What is your favorite food group? How many daily servings do you eat from this group?
2. How many vegetables can you name? Why are vegetables good for you?
3. Why is the dairy group important? How many servings should you eat from this group?
4. What kind of food do people in your country like to eat? Do they like sweets?
5. Do you eat nutritious foods? What foods do you like to eat? What foods don't you like?

FREE RESPONSE

1. What is Ed having for lunch?
2. Is he having a nutritious meal?
3. What do you think Ed should have for lunch?
4. Why are hot dogs and french fries called "junk food"?
5. What are some other examples of junk food?
6. Why do Americans like junk food?
7. Is junk food popular in your country?
8. Do you like junk food?
9. Is junk food good for you? Why or why not?

GROUP WORK • *Plan a nutritious menu for breakfast, lunch, and dinner. Look at the food pyramid on page 136 for ideas.*

· MENU ·		
Breakfast	Lunch	Dinner

WRITTEN EXERCISE • *Listen to the conversation and complete the shopping list.*

Sam, could you get some things at the market for me?

Sure. What do you need?

Shopping List
1 dozen eggs
1 quart of milk

PAIR WORK • *Have similar conversations. Ask your partner to get some things at the market.*

FREE RESPONSE

1. What's your favorite market?
2. What hours is the market open?
3. How long does it take you to do the shopping?
4. Do you ever have to wait in long lines?
5. What kind of food do you buy?
6. Does the market usually have what you're looking for?
7. Are the employees friendly? helpful? courteous?

Listen and practice.

COOKING INSTRUCTIONS • *Listen and repeat.*

1. Slice two potatoes.

2. Sauté in oil 3–4 minutes.

3. Beat six eggs.

4. Add a half cup of milk.

5. Pour mixture over potatoes.

6. Cook 3–5 minutes.

WRITTEN EXERCISE • *Listen to the conversation and write Mabel's recipe for onion soup.*

RECIPE FOR ONION SOUP

1. _____
2. _____
3. _____
4. _____
5. _____
6. _____

PRACTICE • *Make sentences using phrasal verbs with object pronouns.*

> Tino wants to listen to the radio. (turn on)
> **He's turning it on now.**
>
> Mrs. Golo borrowed some books from the library last week. (take back)
> **She's taking them back now.**

1. Barbara got a new computer today. (try out)
2. Peter received some business reports a little while ago. (look over)
3. Barney borrowed some money from Mr. Bascomb a few days ago. (pay back)
4. Mr. and Mrs. Golo have a problem. (talk over)
5. Linda took some books from the living room. (put back)
6. Nancy wants the telephone number of the post office. (look up)
7. Anne is taking her coat from the closet. (put on)
8. Mr. Poole left his children at the park. (pick up)
9. Jack turned on the light in the bedroom. (turn off)

FREE RESPONSE • *Answer the questions using phrasal verbs.*

1. When you don't know the meaning of a word, where do you look it up?
2. When you have a problem, who do you talk it over with?
3. When was the last time you ran into an old friend?
4. How often do you go out on week nights?
5. How often do you go away on weekends?
6. When was the last time you turned down an invitation?
7. When was the last time you put something off?
8. What sport(s) would you like to take up?
9. What famous person do you look up to?

WRITTEN EXERCISE • *Complete the following sentences in your own words.*

> I'm too tired *to play tennis.*
> She's smart enough *to go to college.*

1. He's hungry enough _____

2. She isn't old enough _____

3. It's too hot _____

4. We're too late _____

5. Do you have enough money _____

6. I don't have enough time _____

7. They're too busy _____

8. He's too lazy _____

9. She isn't strong enough _____

TALKING ABOUT YOUR HOMETOWN

1. Where is your hometown?
2. What is the population of your hometown?
3. What are the people like? Are they friendly? hardworking?
4. Is your hometown clean? safe? prosperous? exciting?
5. Is it expensive to live there?
6. How is the weather in your hometown?
7. When is the best time to go there?
8. What are some of the most popular tourist attractions?
9. What are some things you like about your hometown?
10. What are some things you don't like about your hometown?

GROUP WORK • *Discuss your hometown with other students in your class.*

COMPOSITION

1. Write about your hometown. What's it like?
2. Write about an interesting day. Where were you? Who were you with? What happened?

1. _____ people take the bus.
   A. Much   C. A lot of
   B. A little   D. Any

2. They don't have _____ clothes.
   A. much   C. few
   B. some   D. many

3. There's _____ milk in the refrigerator.
   A. a little   C. a few
   B. much   D. many

4. They need some envelopes.
   They don't have _____.
   A. some   C. a few
   B. any   D. much

5. There wasn't _____ traffic on that street last night.
   A. many   C. a little
   B. some   D. much

6. I'm only going to buy _____ stamps.
   A. many   C. a few
   B. much   D. a little

7. Linda _____ go to the market today.
   A. have to   C. need to
   B. has to   D. likes to

8. Nancy _____ speak French.
   A. can to   C. want to
   B. wants   D. can

9. Albert is hungry. He _____ to have dinner now.
   A. can   C. wants
   B. want   D. likes

10. My friends _____ to play tennis.
    A. like   C. can
    B. wants   D. likes

11. Both of those men are tall.
    _____ of them is short.
    A. None   C. All
    B. Neither   D. Some

12. Maria has two radios. _____ of them are good.
    A. Some   C. Both
    B. All   D. One

13. Dr. Pasto has a lot of books.
    _____ of them are very old.
    A. Some   C. Neither
    B. Any   D. Both

14. All of those oranges are ripe.
    _____ of them are green.
    A. Some   C. Neither
    B. Many   D. None

15. There aren't any glasses on the shelf.
    There are _____ on the table, either.
    A. some   C. none
    B. a few   D. any

16. I think _____ took your umbrella.
    A. anyone   C. person
    B. one   D. someone

17. Sam has a lot of friends in Wickam City, but he doesn't know _____ in Colterville.
    A. someone   C. any friend
    B. anyone   D. any person

18. Maria isn't going _____ this weekend.
    A. anywhere   C. somewhere
    B. to anywhere   D. to somewhere

19. She doesn't know _____ about sports.
    A. anything   C. nothing
    B. something   D. none

20. I want to give my brother _____ for his birthday.

    A. a thing   C. anything
    B. something   D. any

21. His friend lives _____ on the other side of town.

    A. near   C. somewhere
    B. here   D. anywhere

22. Barbara doesn't have a car, _____ she takes the bus to work.

    A. as   C. then
    B. because   D. so

23. Jack's always reading books. He _____ like to read.

    A. will   C. would
    B. must   D. can

24. Sam worked hard today. He _____ be tired now.

    A. shall   C. will
    B. can   D. must

25. I hope everyone _____ to the party tomorrow.

    A. will come   C. come
    B. shall come   D. are coming

26. The phone is ringing. _____ I answer it?

    A. Will   C. Shall
    B. Would   D. Won't

27. You look hungry. _____ you like a sandwich?

    A. Will   C. Do
    B. Would   D. Can

28. She's asking _____ some questions.

    A. them   C. for them
    B. to them   D. of them

29. We bought a lamp for Mr. Poole. We gave it _____ last night.

    A. him   C. to her
    B. to him   D. for him

30. Albert likes Linda. He brought _____ some chocolates yesterday.

    A. for her   C. to her
    B. hers   D. her

31. They went _____ after school.

    A. to home   C. home
    B. at home   D. to the home

32. There are some good restaurants _____ Wickam City.

    A. at   C. in
    B. for   D. from

33. The boys are cleaning _____ shoes.

    A. there   C. theirs
    B. their   D. them

34. Is that umbrella _____?

    A. you   C. your
    B. to you   D. yours

35. Where are the glasses? _____ on the shelf.

    A. They're   C. Their
    B. There   D. There are

36. _____ bread in the kitchen.

    A. There are   C. It has
    B. There are some D. There's some

37. She isn't _____ to lift that table.

    A. strong for   C. strong enough
    B. enough strong   D. very strong

38. He's _____ to work.

    A. too lazy   C. lazy enough
    B. very lazy   D. so lazy

39. We _____ dinner when the telephone rang.

    A. was having   C. have
    B. were having D. are having

40. I _____ television when a bird flew into the room.

    A. was watching   C. looked at
    B. were watching D. saw

41. Jimmy and Linda were walking home when they _____ a loud noise.
    A. saw   C. heard
    B. were hearing   D. met

42. Last year at this time Ula Hackey _____ Hollywood.
    A. lived at   C. was living in
    B. was living at   D. is living in

43. Barbara and Tino _____ to the beach last Sunday.
    A. was   C. go
    B. went   D. were

44. Do they often go to the beach?
    Yes, they _____.
    A. do   C. do go
    B. go   D. are going

45. Does Albert have any new magazines?
    No, he _____.
    A. does   C. has
    B. doesn't   D. don't

46. Nancy _____ to play tennis tomorrow.
    A. goes   C. will like
    B. is going   D. likes

47. Your friends aren't going to the post office, _____?
    A. do they   C. they are
    B. aren't they   D. are they

48. Linda was studying last night, _____?
    A. wasn't she   C. she was
    B. she wasn't   D. did she

49. Jimmy took a book from the shelf a few minutes ago. He's putting _____ now.
    A. it on   C. it back
    B. back it   D. them back

50. Gloria is a good dancer. She dances _____.
    A. good   C. very good
    B. goodly   D. well

Preview

Teacher, see page x.

GRAMMAR
Could
Present perfect
Used to

Listen and practice.

Otis **could** paint when he was seven years old.

Anne **could** play the guitar when she was twelve years old.

PRACTICE • *These photographs show some people you know when they were young. Make a sentence for each one using **could**.*

1. **Tino could swim when he was nine years old.**

1. Tino/swim/9

2. Barbara/ski/14

3. Jimmy/play basketball/10

4. Nick/repair cars/15

5. Suzi/dance/8

6. Gloria/cook/11

PAIR WORK • *Ask each other questions using the information under the pictures.*

A: **Could you swim when you were nine years old?**
B: **Yes, I could.**   OR   **No, I couldn't.**

Listen and practice.

In these conversations, the speakers are using the **present perfect.** We often use the present perfect for actions that began in the past and continue up to the present. We form the present perfect with **have/has** + **past participle:**

She's lived here for many years.   I've known her for a long time.

Note: she's = she has   I've = I have

With regular verbs, the past participle has the same form as the simple past:

lived   worked   played

With irregular verbs, the past participle has different forms:

been   had   known

GROUP WORK • *Have similar conversations. Ask these questions and make up your own.*

- How long have you been at this school?
- How long have you studied English?
- How long have you lived . . . ?
- How long have you known . . . ?

Listen and practice.

We often use the **present perfect** to talk about recent events and personal experiences. We are not interested in when these things happened, but only in the fact that they have happened. When we indicate the time of the action, we use the simple past tense.

I've visited Canada.   I visited Canada last spring.

REGULAR VERBS	
live — lived	study — studied
work — worked	dance — danced
play — played	visit — visited

IRREGULAR VERBS	
be — been	meet — met
have — had	see — seen
eat — eaten	take — taken

GROUP WORK • *Have similar conversations. Ask these questions and make up your own.*

- Have you ever been to Paris?
- Have you ever eaten French food?

- Have you ever met a famous person?
- Have you seen any good movies lately?

*We use **used to** when we talk about something that happened in the past but no longer happens.*

When Mr. Lassiter was young, he **used to** have long hair and play pool.

Now Mr. Lassiter has short hair and he plays golf.

PRACTICE • *Make a sentence for each of the old pictures of Mr. Lassiter. Start with* ***He used to*** *+* ***verb***.

1. **He used to have long hair.**

1. _____ long hair.

2. _____ a T-shirt and jeans.

3. _____ a motorcycle.

4. _____ rock music.

5. _____ the guitar.

6. _____ cherry soda.

PAIR WORK • *Talk about things you used to do in the past.*

Appendix

IRREGULAR VERBS

INFINITIVE	PAST TENSE	PAST PARTICIPLE	INFINITIVE	PAST TENSE	PAST PARTICIPLE
be	was	been	lay	laid	laid
become	became	become	lead	led	led
bet	bet	bet	leave	left	left
break	broke	broken	lose	lost	lost
bring	brought	brought	make	made	made
build	built	built	meet	met	met
buy	bought	bought	put	put	put
catch	caught	caught	read	read	read
come	came	come	ride	rode	ridden
cut	cut	cut	run	ran	run
do	did	done	see	saw	seen
drink	drank	drunk	sell	sold	sold
drive	drove	driven	shine	shone	shone
eat	ate	eaten	sing	sang	sung
feed	fed	fed	sit	sat	sat
feel	felt	felt	sleep	slept	slept
fight	fought	fought	speak	spoke	spoken
find	found	found	spend	spent	spent
fly	flew	flown	stand	stood	stood
forget	forgot	forgotten	steal	stole	stolen
get	got	got	swim	swam	swum
give	gave	given	take	took	taken
go	went	gone	teach	taught	taught
grow	grew	grown	tell	told	told
have	had	had	think	thought	thought
hear	heard	heard	understand	understood	understood
hide	hid	hidden	wake	woke	waked
hit	hit	hit	wear	wore	worn
hold	held	held	win	won	won
know	knew	known	write	wrote	written

TAPE SCRIPT FOR PAGE 137

MABEL: Sam, could you get some things at the market for me?

SAM: Sure. What do you need?

MABEL: Well, I need a dozen eggs, a quart of milk, a loaf of bread, some tomato soup, a few oranges, lettuce, toothpaste, and a bar of soap.

SAM: Okay, Mabel, I'll get it for you.

MABEL: Thanks, Sam.

TAPE SCRIPT FOR PAGE 138

MRS. GOLO: Mabel, could you give me your recipe for onion soup?

MABEL: Sure. I was just going to make some when you called. First, slice two onions thinly. Then saute the onions in oil for two minutes. Add a can of chicken broth and season with salt and pepper. Finally, add Parmesan cheese and cook for three to five minutes. It's easy.

MRS. GOLO: Thanks a lot, Mabel.

MABEL: You're welcome.

ask out = invite someone to do something (go to a show, a meal)
He asked her out to a movie.

be against = oppose
I'm against building a toy factory in City Park.

be back = return
I'm going to the drug store. I'll be back in fifteen minutes.

be fed up with = be completely bored
I'm fed up with working. I want to have some fun.

be over = be finished
The meeting will be over in a few minutes.

break into = enter illegally, especially by force (a bank, a building, a house, etc.)
Last month a burglar broke into my apartment and took the TV.

bring up = mention or introduce a subject
You can bring up the question of child care at the next meeting.

call off = cancel (an event, an arrangement, an activity)
We had to call off the picnic because of rain.

catch up with = reach (someone who is ahead)
He was walking fast. I had to run to catch up with him.

cheer up = become happier
My sister was feeling depressed, but she cheered up when you invited her to the party.

come up with = think of, produce (an idea, a plan, a suggestion)
We must come up with a plan to improve the economy.

count on = depend on, rely on (someone)
If you ever need help, you can always count on me.

do without = manage in the absence of a person or thing
I like coffee, but I can do without it.

feel up to = feel strong enough (to do something)
I'm very tired. I don't feel up to playing tennis.

figure out = understand (someone or something) with difficulty
I can't figure out why she married Bill. He has nothing to offer.

fill in = complete (a form, a questionnaire)
It took me fifteen minutes to fill in the application form.

find out = discover after making an effort
How did you find out that she was living in Paris?

get away = escape; be free to leave
The police chased the bandit, but he got away.

get away with = do something wrong or illegal without being punished
She always cheats on her exams. I don't know how she gets away with it.

get back = reach home again
We spent the whole day at the beach and didn't get back until after dark.

get over = recover from (an illness, a shock, a disappointment)
I had the flu last week, but I got over it quickly.

get through = finish, complete (some work, a job, a book)
She had a lot of work to do yesterday, but she got through all of it.

give in = stop resisting; surrender
Her boyfriend didn't want to go dancing, but he finally gave in.

give up = stop trying to do something (often because it is too difficult)
He tried to pick some oranges, but he couldn't reach them so he gave up.

go ahead = proceed; continue
Go ahead. Don't wait for me.

go away = leave; leave this place
Go away! I don't want to see you!

go on = continue any action
Go on with your story. It's very interesting.

go out = go to a social event (as to go to a theater, concert)
She has a lot of friends and goes out a lot.

grow up = become adult
Children grow up very fast nowadays.

hold on = wait (especially on the telephone)
"Hold on. I'll be with you in a minute."

hold up = rob
Two gunmen held up the National Bank last week.

let someone down = disappoint someone (often by breaking a promise or agreement)
You let me down. You promised to help me, but you didn't.

leave out = omit
When he filled out the application form, he left out his phone number.

look after = take care of (someone or something)
My neighbor looks after the dog while I'm away.

look forward to = expect with pleasure
We're looking forward to the party next week.

look someone up = visit someone
She looked up her uncle when she was in San Francisco.

look up to = respect; admire
People look up to Dr. Pasto because of his great knowledge.

make up for = compensate for (a mistake, doing or not doing something)
I'm sorry I forgot your birthday, but I'll make up for it.

move out = leave a house or apartment with one's possessions
Our neighbors moved out of their apartment yesterday.

pick up = get, collect (something or someone)
She picked up a package at the post office.

pick up = give someone a ride in a vehicle
He picked up his girlfriend after work and drove her home.

point out = show; explain
She pointed out that a small car is more practical than a big car.

put back = return; replace (something)
When you finish looking at the magazines, put them back on the shelf.

put off = delay or postpone (doing something until a later time)
Never put off until tomorrow what you can do today.

put up with = suffer; tolerate (a difficult situation or person)
Our neighbors make a lot of noise, and we have to put up with it.

run into = meet someone by chance
I was on my way home when I ran into an old friend.

run out of = use all of and have none left (money, time, patience)
She ran out of money and had to borrow some from me.

see about = make inquiries or arrangements
We called the travel agency to see about getting a flight to New York.

see off = say good-bye to someone who is going on a trip
I saw my brother off at the airport last Sunday.

stand up for = defend verbally
Her mother criticized her, but her father stood up for her.

take off = remove an article of clothing
It was very hot, so he took off his coat.

take over = become the person or group in charge
He took over the business after his father died.

take up = begin a hobby, sport, or kind of study
Last year she took up stamp collecting, and now it's her favorite pastime.

talk over = discuss a matter with someone else
Whenever he has a problem, he talks it over with his wife.

think over = consider carefully (a problem, an offer, a situation)
You don't have to make a decision right away. Go home and think it over.

try on = put on (an article of clothing) to see how it fits
She tried on several dresses before finding one she liked.

try out = test
You should try out the typewriter before buying it.

turn down = refuse, reject (an offer, an application, an applicant)
He applied for a job at the bank but was turned down.

turn out = result, develop, or end
Don't worry. Everything will turn out all right.

turn up/down = increase/decrease (volume, force, pressure)
Would you please turn down the radio? It's too loud.

wear out = use (something) until it is finished
He has worn out three pairs of shoes in the last year.

work out = find the solution to a problem
We don't have enough money to pay all of our expenses, but we'll work things out somehow.

PRONUNCIATION

CHAPTER ONE

uw

fruit	school	movie
juice	newspaper	include
soup	stupid	shampoo
food	student	afternoon

ə

cup	love	young
lunch	money	husband
bus	hungry	subject
truck	study	discuss

Bruce likes fruit juice and soup.
My new shoes are blue.

The bus stop is in front of the drugstore.
Sometimes my brother studies after lunch.

There's a blue truck in front of the school.
Do the students study in the summer?

CHAPTER TWO

p

pan	airplane	happy
peach	hospital	trip
pack	important	sleep
pen	repair	envelope

b

bad	about	table
beach	nobody	club
back	number	job
Ben	husband	cab

The Japanese airplane disappeared over Pakistan.
The passengers planned a party for the pilot.
He painted pretty pictures in the park.

Barney belongs to the Bombay Bicycle Club.
He borrows books from the nearby library.
Nobody knows about the busy cab driver.

Mr. Baker has an important job at the post office.
Perhaps Mabel is at the bus stop.
Albert put the cup by the teapot.

CHAPTER THREE

š

shop	ocean	wash
shame	musician	dish
shower	tradition	brush
sociable	expression	English

tš

chair	kitchen	beach
church	teacher	watch
cheap	picture	French
chocolate	question	sandwich

The short man shined his shoes.
She washed the dishes and took a shower.
Traditional Englishmen often fish in the ocean.

There's a chicken sandwich in the kitchen.
The teacher answered the children's questions.
Charlie Chan has a picture of a Chinese statue.

Miss Shipley played chess with a sociable Frenchman.
She took his cheap Spanish watch.
He chased her across the ocean to China.

CHAPTER FIVE

θ			∂		
think	toothpaste	bath	that	these	another
thank	something	both	them	those	weather
third	anything	fourth	there	father	together
thought	birthday	month	they	mother	neither

Both theaters are on Third Avenue.
I think he'll buy something on Thursday.

They saw their father and mother.
The other brother wasn't there.

My birthday is on the third Thursday of this month.
Those boys told the truth about everything.
They thanked both of their parents.

CHAPTER SIX

a			ə		
fond	pocket	politics	under	money	husband
blond	modern	philosophy	truck	couple	company
cotton	hospital	economy	public	lucky	trouble
concert	strong	belong	come	number	construction

The doctor's blond daughter wants a job at the hospital.
She's fond of hot dogs and pop songs.

The young couple was in front of the truck.
Some hungry customers are coming from the bus.

The public doesn't want another long, hot summer.
The rock concert continued until one o'clock.

CHAPTER SEVEN

b			v		
busy	Cuban	umbrella	vase	clever	drive
bandit	handbag	library	very	never	love
banana	about	club	visit	lovely	leave
borrow	nobody	cab	vegetable	envelope	shave

Mabel's husband is buying a black umbrella.
Nobody borrows money from that bank.
Barney wants bread and butter for breakfast.

They have a very expensive vase.
The clever visitor is leaving the university.
Marvin never shaves in the evening.

Leave the brown envelopes on the table.
Barney never buys vegetables or bananas.
The lovely ballet dancer waved goodbye to the clever bandit.

VOCABULARY

The vocabulary lists include all of the words that appear chapter by chapter in *Exploring English.* Nouns are given in the singular only. Verbs are given in the infinitive form.

Parts of speech have been omitted except for words that can be used as more than one part of speech. These abbreviations are used: adj. = adjective; adv. = adverb; n. = noun; prep. = preposition; v. = verb.

CHAPTER 1

agree	comic book	fun	leaf	okay	practice (v.)
arrive	cost (v.)		lightbulb	only	repairman
	cream	group (n.)	list	or	
bacon		guy	loaf	organ grinder	science
better	describe		low	out	sky
bookshop	dozen	hard (adv.)		owe	snack (n.)
brush		help (n.)	meal	owner	so (conj.)
bucket	else	hobby	medicine		spoon
	everyone		monkey	paint (n.)	sure
cash register		instrument	musical	pastime	
cent	few (adj.)			peanuts	wagon
close (adj.)	few (pron.)	jam (n.)	normally	philosophy	
cloud (n.)	fork			popcorn	
collect	full	lazy	off (prep.)	practice (n.)	

Expressions

Good idea.	In my opinion . . .	Gee.
Practice makes perfect.	Everything else is bad.	Thanks.
How about a little jazz?	Don't be a snob, dear.	It's a shame.
I don't care much for jazz.	Go out and have fun.	She made a new friend.

CHAPTER 2

afterwards	cab	heart attack	must (v.)	save (v.)	tire (n.)
although	cinema	holiday		season	try (v.)
anything		hope (v.)	noise	situation	
anywhere	desperate	however		sleep (v.)	wild
argument	driving (n.)		order (n.)	so (adj.)	winter
		interview		somehow	
balloon	engine		part	something	
beauty salon	expect	just		somewhere	
besides			repair (n.)	spring	
birthday	fall	lecture (n.)	reply (v.)	still (n.)	
briefcase	fight (v.)	loan (n.)	right (adj.)	summer	
	fix up (v.)	loan (v.)	run (v.)		

Expressions

What can I do for you?	What a story!	Have one.	I think so.
Are you employed?	How does it end?	I'd love to.	I don't think so.
Come on.	I just told you.	That's nice of you.	I hope so.
I'm dying to hear about it.	I get it.	My pleasure.	I hope not.

CHAPTER 3

all (pron.)	courteous	flattery	model train	reach	still (adv.)
anything	cupcake			recommend	strength
anywhere		good-looking	neither (pron.)	remember	
apple tart	daisies		none (pron.)	ripe	thought (n.)
author	decide	hardly			
		hear	obvious	saleswoman	voyage (n.)
bag	energy	heavy	one (pron.)	service	
bakery	enough	historical		shopping (n.)	whatever
both (pron.)	exactly		perhaps	size (n.)	which (adj.)
		jacket	pick (v.)	sociable	whole (adj.)
child	fashionable		plan (v.)	somewhere	
compliment	fit (v.)	lift (v.)	pleasant	speaker	

Expressions

Let's see.	Well . . .	May I help you?
Try it on.	Whatever you say.	It isn't worth it.
That's not bad.	That sounds like fun.	Hey!
That looks good on you.	On second thought . . .	hardly ever

CHAPTER 4

advertisement	cool	fast (adv.)	included	nephew	straight
affirmatively	couch potato	frown	inside	neighborhood	suddenly
aggressive	crack (n.)	furnished		nervous	surprised
angrily	criticize		junkyard		sweetheart
anyway	curtain	gang		own	sweetly
attitude	cry	generous	knock		
available		gentle		polite	tenant
awful	dark		laundry	pool	timid
	date (n.)	habit	lead (v.)	positive	T-shirt
bore (v.)	depress	hallway	leader	pull back	
breathe	difficult	hang	leak (n.)		unbelievable
	disgusting	hardworking	location	react	unfurnished
carpet	drip	harmless		rent (n.)	unemployed
ceiling	dumb	hate	manager	rent (v.)	utilities
chest		hide	maybe	rude	
circle	electricity	honest	mean		view
clap	excellent		middle-aged	scare	
complain	exciting	ignore		sharp	wrecked
condition		include	neat	sloppy	
				soon	yell

Expressions

Isn't it a small world?	I'm broke.	Take a look.
I can't wait to see Eddie.	I can't afford to pay.	What for?
It doesn't make any difference.	I'm moving out.	From now on . . .
You're mistaken.	You sure got here fast.	Not at all.
So what?	You don't do your share.	That's too bad.
What about you?	I don't feel like it.	That's what you think.

CHAPTER 5

begin	dance (n.)	favor	lady	reservation	tipping
brochure	deposit (n.)			robber	translate
budget	dine	get away	naturally	romantic	tour (n.)
	distance	grand	next		travel agent
cafeteria	drink (n.)	guide		service	turn off
contest	driver's license		own (v.)	several	
cooking oil		housework		shall	will (v.)
cotton	even		present (n.)	shirt	
cuisine		ideal (adj.)		steak	

Expressions

He's fond of her.   It's on sale.   Not really.

What's for dinner?   No extra charge.   Not right now.

Would you do me a favor?   No problem.   I don't know how.

I'll be happy to.   It's a pleasure.   I'll teach you.

CHAPTER 6

bandit	defend	great	light (n.)	please (v.)	repay
				plenty	respect (v.)
client	entrance	illness	offer (n.)	postpone	
cold (n.)		instead	ounce	pound	safe
common (adj.)	finish (v.)		overweight	probably	should
consider	following (adj.)	knowledge			
court (n.)	frighten		package (n.)	recover	turn down
cute (adj.)		lawyer	place (n.)	refuse	

Expressions

You shouldn't give up.   I'm out of shape.   This is a holdup!   hardly anything

I'll do my best.   Go on a diet.   Right, Mr. Bascomb?   old-fashioned

CHAPTER 7

accident	cause (v.)	fault (n.)	prowler	steal	while (conj.)
ago	choke (v.)	front		sweater	while (n.)
ambulance	copy (n.)		ride (v.)	sweet	
attendant		hit (v.)			
automobile	daily		seat	telephone number	
		must	sharply		
barber	entire		smoke (n.)	unconscious	

Expressions

Stop thief!   It wasn't my fault.

CHAPTER 8

accept	cough (v.)	handful	mayor	protein	sunshine
add	crime	homemade		proud	surrounded
almost	current (adj.)	hometown	natural	pyramid	Swiss
anticipation		hostess	nature		
area	dairy		nutritious	real estate	taste (v.)
attraction	disappointed	if	nuts	recipe	though
average-sized		impression		respect (n.)	top
	east	incredible	open-air	retire	tourism
balance (v.)	election	industry	ordinarily		traffic (n.)
beans	energetic	interest (n.)	outing (n.)	serving	tray
beat (v.)	entertainment	interest (v.)	oven	ski (v.)	
beauty	excellent	invitation		slice (v.)	uncrowded
body			performance	snow (n.)	
bottom	farmland	junk food	photo	snow (v.)	vote (v.)
	feature (v.)		plenty	source	
candidate		land (v.)	pollution	stadium	
certain	green space	left (adj.)	possible	state (n.)	
cooking (n.)			property	station (n.)	

Expressions

Is something wrong?   So far . . .   to take advantage of
I'm concerned about . . .   In many respects . . .   to make a good impression

Maybe next time.
Thanks, anyway.